Ronald L. Capasso
John C. Daresh

The School Administrator Internship Handbook

Leading, Mentoring, and Participating in the Internship Program

CORWIN PRESS, INC.
A Sage Publications Company
Thousand Oaks, California

Copyright © 2001 by Corwin Press, Inc.

All rights reserved. No part of this book may be reproduced or utilized in any form or by any means, electronic or mechanical, including photocopying, recording, or by any information storage and retrieval system, without permission in writing from the publisher.

For information:

Corwin Press, Inc.
A Sage Publications Company
2455 Teller Road
Thousand Oaks, California 91320
E-mail: order@corwinpress.com

Sage Publications Ltd.
6 Bonhill Street
London EC2A 4PU
United Kingdom

Sage Publications India Pvt. Ltd.
M-32 Market
Greater Kailash I
New Delhi 110 048 India

Printed in the United States of America

Library of Congress Cataloging-in-Publication Data

Capasso, Ronald L.
    The school administrator internship handbook: Leading, mentoring, and participating in the internship program / by Ronald L. Capasso, John C. Daresh.
       p. cm.
    Includes bibliographical references (p.   ) and index.
    ISBN 0-7619-7656-6 (cloth: alk. paper)
    ISBN 0-7619-7657-4 (pbk.: alk. paper)
   1. School administrators–Training of–United States–Handbooks, manuals, etc. 2. Interns (Education)–United States. 3. Internship programs–United States–Handbooks, manuals, etc. I. Daresh, John C. II. Title.
   LB1738.5.C36 2000
   371.2'011–dc21
                                          00-009507

This book is printed on acid-free paper.

01 02 03 04 05 06 10 9 8 7 6 5 4 3 2 1

Corwin Editorial Assistant: Kylee Liegl
Production Editor: Nevair Kabakian
Editorial Assistant: Victoria Cheng
Typesetter/Designer: Rebecca Evans

Contents

Acknowledgments   vii

About the Authors   ix

Introduction   1

1. Internships and the Preparation of Educational Leaders   3

    Setting the Stage   3
    Where Do We Go From Here?   8

2. The State of the Art in Internships   9

    Typical Current Practices   10
    Goals and Objectives of Internships   13
    Summary   24

3. Setting the Stage for the Internship   25

    Establishing Internship Goals   25
    Establishing Relationships for a Meaningful Internship Experience   26
    Do You Really Want to Be a School Administrator?   34
    The Internship Project Proposal   35
    Summary   57

4. Leading, Not Simply Surviving   59

    A Suggested Developmental Pattern   60
    Moving Beyond Management Into Leadership   65
    Refining Your Leadership Goal   67
    Summary   68

5. Carrying Out the Internship: Competencies and Skills   69

    The Final Outcome   69
    Guiding the Implementation of an Internship   73

Defining Standards for Internship Practice ... 74
Skill Development Through the Internship Experience ... 82
Educational Leadership Skills ... 82
Resolving Complex Problems ... 83
Communication Skills ... 85
Developing Self and Others ... 85
Summary ... 86

6. The Role of the University Supervisor ... **87**

Periodic Seminars for Interns ... 88
Coordinating the Internship ... 93
Specific Duties of the Supervisor ... 97
Summary ... 100

7. The Field Mentor ... **101**

Characteristics of Effective Field Mentors ... 102
Responsibilities of Field Mentors ... 105
Collaboration Is the Key ... 112
Summary ... 113

8. The Role of the Intern ... **114**

The Intern as Learner ... 116
The Intern as Partner ... 119
The Intern as Reflective Practitioner ... 121
On Being a Reflective Intern ... 126
Summary ... 131

9. Evaluation and Assessment ... **132**

Evaluating the Internship Experience ... 133
Assessing and Evaluating the Effectiveness of the Intern ... 136
University and Field Mentor Evaluations of the Intern ... 149
Summary ... 157

10. After the Internship: What's Next? ... **158**

Lessons Learned ... 159
Summary ... 160
Suggested Reading ... 161

References ... **163**

Index ... **164**

Acknowledgments

In many respects, this book represents the way interns are educated in the Department of Educational Leadership at Rowan University. It is the product of many minds and experiences. Part of it had its genesis in the meticulous and articulate work of Dr. Mario Tomei, Professor Emeritus at Rowan University. More than a decade ago, Dr. Tomei took the time to explore how prospective educational leaders were trained and educated at universities and colleges around the country. From his findings, Dr. Tomei fashioned a unique leadership experience that provided an excellent springboard for the university's current internship program.

Rowan interns from the past 4 years have also had an important impact on making this book a reality. It was through the lens of their internship experiences that we were able to gain a true sense of what interns really need to do in order to have a meaningful learning encounter that ultimately leads to success in actual practice. Their hard work and dedication to wanting to become effective educational leaders must be recognized as a major influence on this work.

We acknowledge the encouragement and support we received from our university colleagues. They fueled our enthusiasm to complete this work.

We also recognize the tremendous value of working with Robb Clouse, Kylee Liegl, Gracia Alkema, and the staff of Corwin Press. It is their professional expertise that is responsible for the final preparation of this work.

We also wish to extend our deepest thanks to Dick A. Flanary, Director of Leadership Development and Assessment at NASSP, and Karen L. Tichy, Associate Superintendent for Instruction of the Archdiocese of St. Louis, for reviewing this work.

Finally, we acknowledge the love, encouragement, and support of Jane, Stephanie, and Bridget. They are the "soul" reasons for wanting to do whatever we do.

Corwin Press extends thanks two reviewers:

Dick A. Flanary
Director of Leadership Development & Assessment, NASSP
Reston, Virginia

Karen L. Tichy, Associate Superintendent for Instruction
Archdiocese of St. Louis, Catholic Education Office
St. Louis, Missouri

—Ronald L. Capasso, Glassboro, New Jersey
—John C. Daresh, El Paso, Texas

About the Authors

Ronald L. Capasso is Associate Professor of Educational Leadership at Rowan University, Glassboro, New Jersey. He has spent 30 years in public school education, having served 12 years as a superintendent of schools in Pennsville, New Jersey, and 5 years as Assistant Superintendent of Schools in Ramsey, New Jersey. He has also served as a consultant and speaker for the U.S. Office of Education, the New Jersey State Department of Education, various government agencies, and numerous school districts. Capasso began his career in education as an Economics and Social Studies teacher in the Pascack Valley Regional High School District, Hillsdale, New Jersey. His doctorate is from Teachers College, Columbia University.

John C. Daresh has spent more than 20 years in higher education, having served as a faculty member or administrator at the University of Texas at El Paso, the University of Northern Colorado, The Ohio State University, and the University of Cincinnati. He has also worked as a consultant and speaker for school districts, universities, and state departments of education across the United States and in England, South Africa, Taiwan, Holland, and Israel. He was a member of the NASSP/Carnegie Commission to Restructure the American High School and has been involved in numerous professional development initiatives sponsored by the National Association of Elementary School Principals. Daresh began his career by working in the public schools of Dubuque, Iowa, and Chicago. His doctorate is from the University of Wisconsin-Madison.

Introduction

The purpose of this book is to provide those who are involved in the preparation of school administrators with an overview of the internship as a central ingredient of effective preservice programs. A critical assumption made throughout the book is that the central goal of such programs is to ensure that those who will step into the roles of assistant principals or principals, or take central office positions and other administrative jobs, should learn what will make them effective leaders, not simply organizational survivors.

For approximately 50 years, the preservice preparation of school administrators in the United States has typically included a requirement for aspiring school leaders to spend at least part of their time "learning by doing." Changes have occurred in university-based programs leading to certification and licensure for school administrators over the years. They have evolved from a few required theory-based courses into full-blown efforts to develop into programs that truly prepare individuals for the challenges of assuming leadership positions. There has been a recognition that leaders are not prepared based solely on the words found in textbooks. In short, the reliance on field-based learning, such as internships, planned field experiences, and other forms of clinical learning, serves as foundations for preservice administrator preparation programs across the country. More than 500 colleges and universities in the United States now provide graduate-level courses designed to prepare people to become school administrators. In nearly every state, some form of intern experience is required for those who wish to lead schools. As a result, there are many individuals each year who enroll in university programs that include a requirement of field-based learning. In this way, educational administration training programs are increasingly like teacher education programs that have required student teaching for many years. For the most part, the administrative internship requires aspiring administrators to work with experienced leaders for a mandated number of hours. It is expected that this contact will result in persons automatically gaining hands-on experience with the skills, knowledge, and competencies identified as critical elements for successful performance as leaders. In many cases, such interning experiences are

1

quite powerful opportunities to learn from skilled practitioners. In some cases, however, future school principals and others learn their craft by watching less-than-competent practice; there simply are times when there are not enough good role models to demonstrate the work to the next generation.

This book is designed to address the issues and practice of internships that can serve as meaningful models for prospective educational leaders. Chapters 1, 2, and 3 relate to organizing and designing a learning encounter that focuses on a realistic set of goals. They provide valuable information that will enable the university, internship site (local school system), and intern to form a bond that enables the partners in the experience to function as a mini-cohort. Chapters 4 and 5 address the specific skills that interns need to extend and enhance during their internship experience in order to prepare to increase the quality of life in the organizations that they will eventually lead. Chapters 6, 7, and 8, speak to the specific roles that the university mentor, field mentor, and intern must enact during the internship experience. Finally, Chapters 9 and 10 address evaluating and assessing the intern and the overall university experience to determine the intern's readiness to step into the world of real practice and serve as an effective leader in the workplace. The book concludes with a list of additional reading that may be considered.

CHAPTER 1

Internships and the Preparation of Educational Leaders

From the Field 1.1

Good Knight

When Charlie Mae Knight was appointed the new superintendent for the Ravenwood School district in East Palo Alto, California, she was the 12th superintendent in 10 years. She encountered a district in which 50% of the schools were closed and 98% of the children were performing in the lowest percentile for academic achievement in California. The district had the state's lowest revenue rate. There were buckets in classrooms to catch the rain leaking through decrepit roofs, the stench from the rest rooms was overwhelming, homeless organizations were operating out of the school sites, and pilfering was rampant. Gophers and rats had begun to take over the facilities. As if this weren't challenging enough, Knight had to wrestle with a lawsuit that had gone on for 10 years, the intent of which was to dissolve the district for its poor educational quality and force the children to transfer to schools outside of their community (Kouzes & Posner, 1995).

Setting the Stage

Our nation's schools are complex organizations and growing more so all the time. This phenomenon is taking place because of the constant demand for significant, albeit traumatic, reforms in the way schools do things to achieve desired outcomes. Some of these demands emanate from two distinct sources of influence. One is the globalization of society and the coming of the information age. The other is the changing attitudes of local societal factions toward the institution of education.

Our youth must graduate from schools that have prepared them to learn and survive in a global society. Students must be prepared to be their own global learning organization. They must understand that acquiring knowledge rapidly and competently is essential to all learning. They must be able to apply such knowledge to complex, multicultural societal challenges. If students are unable to do this, they will be doomed to failure. It can be projected that a majority of the membership of any kindergarten class will be working at jobs and producing products that might not be created and developed until well after they have graduated from high school. Their school must properly educate them for that eventuality.

There was a time when schools were filled with students who were motivated to learn. Their parents were fully supportive of the school district's teachers and administrators. The community at large routinely supported the annual school budget. The state and federal governments encouraged research and change through the passage of special legislation. It was a time when school administrators were considered major community leaders. It was a time when educators enjoyed the respect and partnership of the entire community.

Times have changed, however. No longer can educators depend on children coming to school with a genuine respect for learning. No longer can they depend on parents' supporting school district policy and building regulations. No longer can they assume that a school budget will pass without critical opposition. No longer can they depend on the generosity of government to fund experimentation. Perhaps worst of all, no longer can they assume that the community partnership they need to be successful will be there for the right reasons. The results of these deficiencies can be witnessed in Charlie Mae Knight's situation.

If you are currently connected to a public school district (or have a close working knowledge of one), take a few moments to list some of the major changes and the corresponding results that have occurred over the past 5 years (e.g., perhaps your district always enjoyed community support for its annual budget, but over the past several years budgets have been voted down, causing a reduction in support for advance placement programs at the high school).

Change	*Result*
_____	_____
_____	_____
_____	_____
_____	_____

As you reflect on these changes and results, envision the role educational leadership played in either bringing about the change or affecting the results. Furthermore, try to remember how school administrators addressed the results. In your mind, did they do an effective job? Why or why not?

Sometimes changes that have a negative effect on schools are as much the result of ineffective leadership as they are a result of the actions of other societal factions.

From the Field 1.2

Tradition Can Reign Supreme

The Fairhaven School District historically enjoyed an excellent relationship with the community. Through its efforts, a number of traditional annual events had been established for its students. One of these events was the annual trip taken by elementary classes to various sites in the area.

In 1989, the state government informed the Fairhaven School District that it would loose a significant amount of financial aid. Loss of this aid created a 63-cent school tax increase to the homeowners of Fairhaven. In 1989, Fairhaven School District suffered its first budget defeat in 15 years. Immediately after the election, Superintendent Jones called a meeting of her principals to discuss the effect of the election on the next year's planned activities.

After a lengthy meeting it was decided that since there were 2½ months to go in the current school year, all administrators would rethink their current-year needs to see if any significant dollars could be rerouted (with approval from the board of education) to purchase some of the programs for the next year. In making this decision, it was further decided that money set aside for the current year's traditional elementary class trips would be kept on hold until such time as the district's financial condition was brought into balance. (There was never any discussion that the trips would be cancelled.)

Upon returning to his school building, Principal Smith decided to call a faculty meeting to inform them of how the district was going to handle the unexpected financial shortfall. He held the meeting the following morning before school began. In his deliberation, he mentioned the possibility of not having the annual class trips in order to save money. The staff was surprised, but supported the idea since they did not like having to take the trips.

In his zeal to cover all the bases, at the end of the school day Principal Smith made the following announcement to the entire student body: "Because next year's budget was voted down, there will be no class trips this year." Needless to say, the next day Principal Smith's telephone rang off the hook with calls from parents. As he spoke to parents, he dutifully referred them to Superintendent Jones.

Superintendent Jones made every attempt to explain that the decision was not to cancel the trips, but to consider the financial condition of the district in light of the budget defeat. As it turned out, the board of education was able to address a reasonable budget reduction plan without canceling the class trips. However, the parents never forgot the "attempt on the part of the school district administration to retaliate a budget defeat by hurting children and cutting out the *traditional* class trips that had been in the district since its beginning." They saw the return of the trips as a result of their pressure, not as a result of the board and administrators' ability to resolve a financial problem.

To date, the district has not recovered from this administrative error. Principal Smith's poor timing, lack of understanding of community tradition, and lack of communication with Central Office created an issue that has become a major factor in the past 10 defeated budgets of the Fairhaven School District.

If school reform (including a revival of community and government support for education) is to be successful, it will be largely as a result of the reformation of the image of educational leaders. Leaders must be effective if they are to participate in any reform movement. These leaders must be individuals who define their role through the eyes of their followers. The followers must see their leaders as role models who are willing to accept their responsibilities to do the right things and achieve results. The leaders must know and/or know how to define the needs of their district or building, and know what they have to do to make a difference in addressing those needs.

Take a moment to think about the person who is your current superintendent or principal. (If you are not currently active in a school district, think of those individuals for whom you have worked in the past. You can also use Superintendent Jones and/or Principal Smith in From the Field 1.2.) List some of the characteristics that you believe make this person an effective leader and the results of that effective leadership. Also, list some characteristics that you believe make this person an ineffective leader and the results of that ineffectiveness. (For example, you may work for a principal who has effectively played the role of an instructional leader, which has resulted in an excellent building response to a districtwide curriculum mandate. On the other hand, the same person might have difficulty in dealing with concerned parents, which has resulted in complaints to the Board and/or central office and lackluster participation in the P.T.A.)

Characteristic of Effectiveness   *Result*

_____   _____

_____   _____

_____   _____

_____   _____

Characteristic of Ineffectiveness	*Result*

For some time now, the effort to educate individuals to become effective educational leaders has been going in a very positive direction. More than 500 colleges and universities now have preservice programs that include a requirement that aspiring school administrators spend at least part of the time "learning by doing." These preservice programs have evolved from memorizing textbook theory, to taking theory to practice through the use of internships, planned field experiences, practica, or other forms of formal clinical learning. Such experiences can make an extreme difference when you consider that educational leaders are faced with the real possibility of having to take over a district situation like the one Charlie Mae Knight did. Or they may find themselves in a situation such as Principal Smith, where understanding the culture of a community and its impact on administrative decision making could mean the difference between being viewed as a deceptive person or an effective leader.

These internship experiences should be designed to be meaningful and highly professional learning experiences. They should be meant to provide for a long-term evaluation of a student's leadership ability in a school setting by those practicing professionals who are most experienced in those settings. They should provide educational leadership students with an opportunity to experience the charted and uncharted day-to-day occurrences at the building and district levels. In addition, they should provide opportunities for these students to observe and experience how leadership addresses broader based problems such as reopening closed schools, maintaining facilities, dealing with the public at large, and convincing taxpayers to support educational budgets. There is no doubt that well-organized internships can play an important role in the education of effective school leaders.

This book provides a guideline for how to plan, conduct, and evaluate well-organized internship experiences. A well-organized internship program accomplishes a number of important goals for three different populations. For the *intern* it is an opportunity to self-assess leadership ability at a point of action. It also challenges an intern's commitment to becoming a full-time educational leader. It helps answer the question, "Am I making the right career decision?" For the *university faculty member* who is in charge of mentoring interns, it provides an extreme opportunity to assess the student's ability to take theory to practice. It also provides an opportunity to assess the effectiveness of the entire preservice program in the preparation of future educational leaders. Furthermore, it provides an opportunity to participate in a community outreach program with active school districts. This is especially true if interns are participating in the solution of real problems confronting the sponsoring school district. It is felt that the intern is providing valuable service to the school district through the university preservice program. Finally, for *field mentors* it provides a clear understanding of what their role should be in facilitating the intern's success. In conjunction with the intern's willingness to learn and to work hard, it is the field mentor's professional know-how and knowledge of the school district and community cultures that ensures the intern's ultimate success.

Where Do We Go From Here?

This book is organized around five staging areas of well-designed and -implemented internships. Chapters 2, 3, and 4 focus on initializing an internship through discussions relating to goal setting, designing strategies, and the relationship of the internship to leadership development. Chapter 5 focuses on the implementation of an internship and the development of leadership competencies and skills. Chapters 6, 7, and 8 deal with the role function of the primary participants in an internship. The specific role responsibilities and expectations of the intern, university mentor, and field mentor are discussed and interrelated. Chapter 9 discusses how to evaluate the progress and final accomplishments of an intern, as well as the internship experience. Finally, Chapter 10 peers into the future and makes suggestions as to the types of activities that an intern should participate in beyond the internship experience.

Throughout this book, there are a number of opportunities to participate in activities essential to the development of a well-organized internship. These activities are provided to afford the reader a chance to preplan and carry out a successful internship experience.

CHAPTER 2

The State of the Art in Internships

From the Field 2.1

Mary Farnsworth had spent the past 3 years working on her state administrative certificate by taking courses at Mt. Maxwell State University. Virtually every Tuesday and Thursday night, she would finish her work as a fourth-grade teacher in Clearwater Falls and drive 20 miles over to Mt. Maxwell, find a parking space, and dash in for whatever class she was taking that term. Finally, she had gotten to the point where she could say she would complete all the requirements for a master's degree in educational leadership and the state principalship certificate. The only thing left on her program of studies was the administrative internship.

The general word among classmates was that the internship at Mt. Maxwell was just one more hoop to jump through. As one of her best friends, who had gotten the principalship certificate last year, had told her, "All you do is sign up for the course, pay another fee, go back to your school and have the principal sign a form that shows that you spent some time 'playing principal.' If there is a lot that the principal needs done that term, you might have to sit in the office and help with answering the phones now and then, or you might help with the textbook inventory in the spring like I did. It's no big deal, and you'll get a good grade when you get this thing out of the way."

Mary appreciated the insights because she knew that she would not be under a lot of stress in the internship. Still, she wished that there might be a little more to the internship. After all, it might be her last chance to get ready to do the work of being a principal.

Shortly after World War II there was an awareness in the United States that there would likely be a need for an increasing number of individuals who would be prepared to step into administrative positions around the nation.

The post-War baby boom meant the arrival of many more children, and therefore a need for more schools. With more schools came the automatic need for more people to assume positions as principals and assistant principals. As a result, the number of universities involved with school administrator preparation across the country increased to more than 500 by 1960.

With the advent of more administrator preparation programs came another realization: Many university-based programs simply were not doing a very good job of enabling people to acquire the requisite knowledge and skills for the principalship. The primary reason for this was that graduate programs were said to emphasize the theory of administration rather than the practice. Therefore, it was noted that a critical need existed for finding aspiring administrators to acquire the practical skills associate with their chosen field.

The result of this is the emergence of what has become a relatively standard practice in most states across the country. There is a requirement that those who plan on pursuing managerial positions in schools spend at least a portion of their preservice education learning in the field so they will know more about the daily demands and responsibilities of school leaders. At present, the expectation that future administrators engage in an internship, planned field experience, or some similar form of practicum has become standard practice in all but a handful of those states where administrators must qualify for a state certificate or license.

Simply acknowledging that most future administrators must complete some form of internship does not present a full picture of what it means to "learn by doing." In this chapter, we present a brief overview of the internship as an instructional practice used as part of principal preparation programs across the country. We begin by looking at the characteristics of "typical" internship programs currently in place at universities across the United States. You may wish to consider the ways in which the program in which you are now participating matches these features. Second, we will present some of the long-standing assumptions of potential outcomes of the administrator preparation internship. As you read through this review of field-based learning related to school administrator preparation, you may wish to think about the ways in which you are achieving some of the potential benefits noted here. If you are not already addressing some of these issues, you may wish to consider how your current experience can become more effective and satisfying to you in learning how to lead and manage a school.

Typical Current Practices

Because the internship has recently been identified as a critical part of more effective school administrator preparation, literature on this topic provides a fairly well-defined picture of what the typical practicum looks like. We reviewed descriptions of the characteristics of the field-based components of more than 40 universities across the United States and discovered the following general features related to program design:

- Typical field-based programs are not required of all students enrolled in educational administration degree programs, but rather only of students seeking a license or administrator certificate from an agency external to the university. Further, most activities, when required, occur toward the end of students' academic programs.

What this means is that, in many states, university programs in educational administration are designed to serve multiple audiences. While they may appear to be designed primarily to prepare people to step into roles as school principals or assistant principals, the fact is that master's degree programs in educational administration often attract students who have little or no interest in serving as school administrators. As a consequence, internships are often add-ons designed specifically for those who want to be certified in a particular state. The implication for you may be that you are proceeding through a university program that does not necessarily have a clear focus on preparing people to step into school leadership positions. If that is the case, the internship may be an even more critical part of your program, since it is clearly designed to help people refine practical skills needed in the field.

The second characteristic of most university intern programs, namely that they are required at the end of students' programs, also represents an unfortunate reality. In many cases, the one time during a preservice program that you can actually go into a school and "taste" what it means to be an administrator is so late in your academic program that you are not likely to decide *not* to go into administration. After all, if you have already completed the bulk of the coursework needed to get a degree or certificate in administration, you will have spent a lot of time and money in pursuing a career in this field. It is unlikely that near the end of such a program and investment you will suddenly decide to go down a different path. If this describes a situation that you face in your program, it may be wise to find other ways earlier in your program to explore the real world of school administration more carefully. Whether requirements of classes or not, interview current administrators, observe the behavior of principals and assistant principals, and visit leaders in many different schools. In short, work to answer the critical question: "Is this a life that I want to lead if I leave the classroom?"

- Most internship programs operate in basically the same fashion: Students are expected to register for an academic credit-bearing course called "administrative internship," "planned field experience," or some similar title and spend anywhere from 10 to 40 hours per week during a term observing a practitioner who, in turn, assigns the student some task or project to be carried out under his or her supervisor.

Perhaps the biggest lesson to be considered based on this observation is that, in order to learn the most that you can during an internship, you need to approach this learning experience with a clear plan. If you do not have a set of objectives related to the internship, you are likely to discover that the internship experience will become little more than a time to assist a principal in carrying out tasks that he or she does not want to do. You can easily fill your required 75, 150, or 300 hours of mandated internship time doing office tasks alone. Remember that your overall goal should be to gain deep insights as quickly as possible into the full range of activities associated with being a principal.

- Field-based programs normally provide academic credit, but student evaluation is of the pass/fail variety. The responsibility for evaluating student performance most often resides with the university faculty member who coordinates the practicum.

Regardless of how your university evaluates, or grades, the internship in which you are now enrolled, remember that the most important assessment lies in your hands as you work with your university supervisor and your mentor administrator in the field. The internship focus must ultimately be assessed on the extent to which you personally achieve and learn what you believe you need to learn. Regardless of whether you get an "A" or a "Passing" grade in the course titled "Internship," the experience will be judged as a quality activity if it is successful for you as a learner.

- The university faculty supervisor or coordinator is usually the only faculty member in the department of educational administration who works with students in the practicum. Other faculty often are not actively involved in supervising practica. In many institutions, the person responsible for supervising internships is not a regular faculty member, but rather an adjunct clinical instructor.

The implication for you, if your university follows this model, is that you need to work very directly with the person who is in charge of the intern program, perhaps more than you might with other members of the university faculty who are responsible for traditional courses such as law, supervision, finance, and so on. The university supervisor of the administrative internship has a very distinct and difficult role, namely to work with you in bringing together the world of theory and the world of practice. If the supervisor or coordinator has recently moved into the university from a position as a practicing school administrator, he or she has the opportunity to have a significant impact on your professional development.

- The duration of most internships is normally dictated by the length of the university's academic term, not the time required to complete the assigned field experience.

Regardless of whether your internship is said to be "finished" simply because the semester or quarter has ended or because you have completed the number of mandated hours in the field, you may wish to consider the importance of staying with a field project to see it to its natural conclusion. That will be part of your duty as an administrator in the real world. After all, principals do not simply "lock up the school" and go home in the middle of a crisis. You might as well begin to appreciate the need to follow through before you get a formal administrative assignment, even if the structure of the internship does not require this type of commitment.

- Students enrolled in internships are typically not paid for their work. As a result, most administrative interns today are involved on a part-time basis while attempting to continue with teaching or other professional responsibilities in the same schools where they are engaged in their practice.

In other words, you are far from being alone if you are trying to juggle your daily teaching assignment with attempting to spend time acquiring insights and skills as an administrator. Most people face the same challenges that you do. Having said that, however, you should still try to find ways to spend time away from your present setting, visiting other administrators on their campuses and working to gain insights into levels of schools in which you do not currently work. Using personal leave days or visiting other sites after your workday has concluded might be a way for you to break away from the constraints that you face as a person not able to spend all your time learning about administration.

Goals and Objectives of Internships

A central part of the preparation of teachers has been the student teaching experience normally required as one of the last activities before receiving licensure or certification. Here, aspiring teachers are immersed in their new profession by spending a period of time living the life of a classroom teacher on a full-time basis. Turney (1982) described this activity by noting,

Ideally conceived the practicum is a powerful series of professional experiences in which student teachers apply, refine, and reconstruct theoretical learnings, and through which they develop their teaching competence. The practicum is an integral part of the program of teacher education contributing to the achievement of its aims and closely related to its content competence.

Unlike teachers, administrators are not expected to convey "content competence." There are few "correct answers" when it comes to providing leadership in a school. As a result, there is much to be learned in an administrative internship, but not in the same way that a person learns how to teach mathematics, social studies, or science. Further, as we noted earlier, there is a huge difference between learning about a career as a teacher (frequently as a full-time undergraduate student) and learning how to be an administrator (typically as a part-time graduate student). Despite these major differences, however, administrative internships can have very positive outcomes. Well-designed programs offer participants many possible alternative goals:

1. Enable interns to develop administrative competence progressively through a range of practical experiences

2. Allow interns to apply knowledge and skills gained through universities in a practical setting

3. Enable interns to test their personal commitment to a career

4. Provide interns with an opportunity to gain insights into the preparation of a school, its goals, and how those goals may be achieved

5. Give interns insights into their progress toward personal and professional goals

6. Showcase the talents of interns as potential future school leaders

Let us go over each of these possible outcomes in greater detail, and then consider some ways in which you might be able to address each during your internship.

Developing Administrative Competence

Developing administrative competence is viewed as the traditional core goal of any internship. Here, interns are given the opportunity to get out into the real world where they can get practical experience with actual issues faced regularly by school administrators.

In the past, this form of learning might have been accomplished by releasing promising teachers from their classroom assignments so they could learn how to be a principal by watching a more experienced person at work. This was the closest thing to an apprenticeship program that existed in the field of educational administration. In the earliest days of preparing people to become school administrators, there was no established curriculum to be followed for preservice training. In fact, well-defined university-based programs in educational administration are relatively recent developments. Learning how to manage a school used to be left up to an individual staff member who was expected to teach classes and, with a small amount of released time, also engage in the oversight and coordination of the schoolhouse.

Learning how to administer was often a case of "learning while doing" for people suddenly thrown into a managerial position. As schools became more complex, educational administration finally became a full-time job. The norm was for people to go directly from classrooms into principalships with little or no formal preparation. It was not until the second half of the 20th century that school districts and state education agencies began to adopt required programs of preservice training for administrators. These programs were designed to ensure quality administration by mandating instruction in various aspects and functions of administration for those who had experience as teachers but not as managers. The model followed was similar to that for preparing classroom teachers, with the exception that programs in educational administration were envisioned mostly as post-baccalaureate learning experiences open only to those who had already developed competence in classrooms.

As the majority of modern school administrators moved into their offices armed with knowledge obtained through newly developed programs in school management, it became increasingly apparent that while people were learning *about* administration in university classes, they had problems translating theory into practice. People were still walking into their jobs relatively unprepared because they had not really learned *how* to administer. As this situation grew worse, a solution was proposed to require a period of practical, field-based learning as part of the preservice program for future administrators. The reasoning was simple: If future teachers are required to engage in a period of learning through student teaching, then why not also require those who were to become principals to learn in the same way? The rationale was easy to understand: Watching over the shoulder of an experienced leader is a critical part of one's preparation for the job.

It is easy to appreciate how the first and most obvious objective of internships comes quickly to mind when thinking about what interns learn. For years, intern learning has been directed toward the development of administrative competence in real-world settings.

As a way to help you get the most out of this potential outcome of an administrative internship, we suggest that you take a moment to consider the nature of administrative competencies you wish to learn. There are many lists of skills and knowledge that have been mandated either by state certification policies, school district requirements, or the policies of the institution in which you are enrolled for your internship. Here, we are not asking you to list those assigned skills. Rather, take a moment to reflect on the following question: "If you became a principal or assistant principal tomorrow, what skills associated with that job now cause you the greatest apprehension because you lack confidence in your ability to carry out those duties in a school?" List some of the things that you believe you need to learn during your internship.

_____

_____

_____

_____

_____

The internship, of course, is a time when you are able to demonstrate your ability to perform duties and tasks assigned to you. More important, however, we believe that an effective intern experience should be a time for you to identify your strengths and your limitations so that you can fine tune your leadership skills in a real-world setting. This is your opportunity to learn how to administer and how to blend the world of theory acquired through university courses with the world of practice.

Applying Theoretical Knowledge in Practice

The development of administrative skill is a matter of being able to blend ideas with action. In other words, having good ideas is certainly part of becoming an effective leader, but ideas without implementation are not sufficient. On the other hand, acting without thought is not a skill and not what you are being trained to do.

People learn in a variety of ways and by acquiring different forms of knowledge. Ann Hart (1990) identified three types of knowledge that can be consulted by educational leaders as a way to guide practice.

Experiential Knowledge. This is knowledge gained directly from the outcomes of actions taken personally in similar circumstances and indirectly by talking with others who have had similar experiences. Some call this "craft knowledge" because it reflects the ability to learn as a result of gaining experience with a variety of typical (and often, nontypical) situations that arise in the course of an administrator's workday.

Empirical Knowledge. This is knowledge that aspiring administrators encounter in university study. It is based on evidence systematically collected and analyzed. If schools functioned with the same degree of predictability that we expect when studying the physical sciences, this form of knowledge would be extremely useful because it might present a "blueprint" for administrators to follow in their problem-solving duties. Unfortunately, it is rare that empirical findings are so clear that principals know how to proceed because "research proves" that certain things will happen when data are manipulated in a certain way.

Theoretical Knowledge. This is knowledge based on theories that "search for new facts, [try to] establish their relationships to existing knowledge, and explain generally observed phenomenon" (Hart & Bredeson, 1996, p. 23). Professors build their courses on such knowledge bases. Practitioners rarely believe that theories hold water, much less the solutions to real problems.

An important part of an effective internship can be the effort to bring together these three types of knowledge, all of which have the potential of helping you deal with the complex issues faced by school administrators. The important skill to be acquired through experiential learning is to be able to determine ways in which each form of knowledge listed above can be enhanced by the others. For example, theoretical knowledge shows how people *ought* to be motivated in certain situations. Observations of actual behavior in the field (empirical knowledge) modify the nature of the theory. Developing a program of staff motivation based on empirical research contributes to overall effective practice. The key to consistent effective practice lies in being able to do this on a regular basis. Your internship is an ideal setting for this type of thinking and acting to occur.

Let us take a look at some ways in which you might be able to begin responding to the combination of theoretical, empirical, and experiential model to assist you as a leader.

1. Consider two or three ideas that you have read or heard about in your graduate studies. These should be ideas that intrigue you, interest you, or otherwise cause you to think further about some topic on which you have not really concentrated in the past (e.g., the ways in which decisions are made by administrators). List one or two of these general, theoretical ideas in which you have some interest.

_____

_____

_____

_____

2. Next, make use of empirical research by thinking of some ways in which you could research the theories you have identified (e.g., if you are interested in how principals make decisions, you could go to meetings where the principal must make several decisions and observe the behavior shown in that setting).

---

3. Now, develop a plan for learning more about the theoretical principles, refined by research, in the kind of real-life setting in which you will engage as an administrative intern (e.g., you may attend several meetings involving the principal and several different groups such as teachers, parents, students, or other administrators. Note how decisions are made in these different groups).

You have now looked at a particular issue through the multiple lenses provided by three different forms of "knowing." As a result, you may have identified several additional issues that you could analyze and understand more about by considering the theory, subjecting it to testing and research, and, finally, looking at examples of it in the field.

Testing Personal Commitment

Pursuing an administrative career means that you have invested time and money trying to find a leadership role in schools. You have purchased books, paid tuition, and spent many hours away from home and family studying and attending courses. Simply stated, there is a question you must still answer: "Is administration really the direction in which I want to go in my career as an educator?" You may not know the answer until you begin to practice as a school administrator.

The internship serves as a good transitional experience that may assist you to step from the world of the classroom teacher to the world of the administrator's office. In addition to the benefits we have already reviewed, the internship should also be seen as a way to test your own commitment to a field that you have read about and seen from the classroom. Now, with an effective intern experience, you will have data to help you answer the critical question, "Do I really want to do what I am are being trained for?"

This is not only a time when you may check to see if you have the skills needed to manage a school. There are also many technical aspects to the role of the administrator. You must know certain laws and policies, be able to balance a budget, communicate effectively, and demonstrate a range of competencies associated with effective management. But there is an even more critical issue to be considered, and now is the time to do it. The issue is whether or not you want to do the job now that you are able to see what it consists of "up close and in person." School administrators must perform a large number of tasks each day as part of their assigned duties, and some of those things might not be things that you would wish to do on a daily basis. For example, principals work primarily with adults. If you are currently a classroom teacher, the primary focus of your work is students. To be sure, teachers work with you, and you must make contact with secretaries, custodians, and other support personnel from time to time, but the principal works primarily with those with whom you probably have only sporadic contact. Research (Lortie, 1975) has shown that one of the major attractions to people entering teaching is the fact that they like to work with young people. In all probability, as a classroom teacher, that is still a compelling reason for you to come to work each day. The fact is that when you step out of the classroom and into an administrative office, you are going to be stepping away from one of the prime reasons for your choice of career as an educator. Principals, of course, still have contact with students, but it is often very different from the kind of interaction that takes place daily between teachers and students. Are you ready to make that change?

Numerous other responsibilities go with the role of school administrator. For example, principals and assistant principals need to reprimand and discipline other adults from time to time. In fact, they may even have to terminate a person from a position. Will that be the type of duty you can handle? What about innumerable meetings? Calming hysterical parents? Meeting seemingly impossible deadlines? These are some of the many aspects of administrative life that may be inconsistent with what you want to do in your career.

As you plan your internship, what are some of the issues that you want to explore to determine if you have chosen the right path? For example, how are the responsibilities for evening and weekend supervision likely to fit in with your lifestyle? List other similar issues that you will consider while serving as an intern.

_____

_____

_____

_____

After you have reflected on the issues you have identified above and then compared them with what you discover are the realities of life as an administrator, you are still likely to have many difficult decisions to make. On the one hand, you have already invested much in pursuing your goal in administration. On the other hand, you will need to think seriously about whether or not the potential conflicts and discrepancies that you face can be addressed in a way that will make your career as a future administrator successful.

Insights Into a School

A fourth potential outcome to be derived through the administrative internship concerns your ability to gain greater insights into how the school, as an organization, can be prepared so it is possible for important goals and objectives to be achieved by a student. The traditional focus of internships has been on helping individual interns acquire skills needed to ensure that they will be ready to step into an administrative post. In addition, it is also possible to make the internship a way for interns to look outward, toward the school, and use the experience as a way to learn more about the organization in which they will work.

A common feature of schools is that at the beginning of each school year goals and objectives are established for the students and staff of that school to achieve. It is desirable for you, as an intern, to be there at the point in the school year during which those goals are set for the school in which you will work. A critical skill for anyone in a present or future leadership role is knowing how to work with staff in formulating organizational goals. It may not always be possible to be in a school while this process is actually taking place. It is always possible to look at the goals that have already been developed and spend time with those who were involved with their development to learn how the process took place.

After goals have been developed for a school, the next thing to learn are the strategies used to help staff achieve these stated goals. As an intern in a school, even for only part of a year, it will be possible to watch this process emerge. While you may not have witnessed the entire continuum of goal development, you can at least observe the ways in which people attempt to reach standards they have set.

In the space below, write out two or three of the goals that you have watched being developed for the school in which you are serving as an intern. If you are not able to watch that process, identify two or three issues that have been set by the staff for the next school year. Next, indicate the strategies that have developed as a way for staff to achieve the stated goals.

Goals:

_____

_____

_____

_____

_____

_____

_____

Strategies to be followed to achieve the goals:

_____

_____

_____

_____

_____

_____

_____

Finally, while the goals and strategies may have been devised without your direct involvement, you have an opportunity to make a personal contribution to help your school while you serve as an intern. In the space below, indicate some of the ways in which you believe you can make a contribution to your school by assisting with the strategies or goals listed above.

_____

_____

_____

_____

_____

_____

_____

_____

_____

Gaining Insights Into Professional Development

One more objective to be attained through your internship involves the acquisition of insights into your own progress in personal and professional development. The assumption is that you have consciously been charting your developmental needs as you have progressed through your preservice preparation program. Unfortunately, many people do not pay enough attention to this aspect of becoming an educational leader. However, even if you have not been purposefully charting your own progress, the internship can be an excellent time for you to develop the habit of checking on where you stand in your career.

Most interns are required to keep a record or log of activities in which they are engaged during the course of the internship. The expectation is generally that interns document the specific activities that they are involved in and then relate these activities to the broad competencies or goals of the overall program. Another purpose for keeping detailed logs is that they enable the university supervisor or coordinator to assess whether or not interns have invested the requisite hours in the field during a school term. States typically require interns to spend anywhere from 50 to 300 hours engaged in administrative activities, and the log enables reviewers to see if students have met this mandate.

We propose, in addition to the log of activities, that it is good practice to check personal and professional growth by also maintaining a diary while in the field. Where the log documents the completion of tasks, the diary is a personalized record of your perceptions of how much you have learned as a result of engaging in the activities. The diary can be a completely confidential document, not subject to any supervisory review. Instead, it should be something that enables you to look at how far you have grown as a future administrator after carrying out certain practices in a school.

Ideally the diary will provide you with an opportunity to compare what you have personally learned in the field against a set of predetermined personal goals and objectives that you specified before starting your internship. If you have not already done so in another format, use the space below to write down the personal professional goals that you hope to achieve as a result of participating in the internship. These should be different from any required outcomes expected of everyone who goes though this same learning experience. These should be broad goals, not simply a list of specific skills that you want to learn more about. The opportunity to list those skills will be presented in greater detail in Chapter 4.

For example, the state may require you to spend a certain amount of time in preparing documents used in communicating with parents or community groups. In your own mind, you may wish to refine your writing skills during this next year so that you will be able to convey important ideas to different audiences with which you will work as an administrator.

———————————————————————

———————————————————————

———————————————————————

———————————————————————

———————————————————————

———————————————————————

———————————————————————

As you progress with the entries in your diary during your internship, you may find it helpful to ask another person–someone we might call a "critical friend"–to read over writings periodically to give you some feedback. While it is helpful to review your own personal progress, it is even more useful to have someone else review your perceptions from time to time. The person who engages in this activity should not be someone who will be involved with evaluating your performance of required skills. Rather, you should feel comfortable enough with your critical friend to be able to write honestly and openly as you proceed through the year, without the fear of a lower grade regarding the content of your diary entries.

Showcasing Talent

The final outcome of an administrative internship centers on the fact that this experience is likely to serve as a way for you to learn about the field, but even more important for your career, for the field to learn about you and your talents. During the internship you will suddenly begin to be noticed by others as a person who has some interest in the world of school administration. This does not automatically mean that, by serving as an intern, you will suddenly be deluged with offers of an administrative position. On the other hand, until you proactively move toward increasing visibility and an assumption of more responsibility, you will be only one of many hundreds of staff members in a district.

Over the years, we have frequently suggested to interns that they look for opportunities to go beyond the minimum requirements of the field experience. Specifically, interns should actively seek opportunities to get out of the buildings where they spend most of their time. There are two reasons for this. First, by going from your primary setting, you will be able to see and learn about practices in other environments. Second, and perhaps even more important, is the fact that by working in multiple settings you will come into contact with many other administrators who will get to "check you out" as a prospective colleague.

The internship is a way for you to become acquainted with how you feel as an administrator. In addition, the internship is also an important way for others to get acquainted with how you look to them as an administrator.

Summary

This chapter began with a brief overview of some of the characteristics of administrator internships that have been found at the majority of universities with administrator preparation programs. Then six alternative possible objectives for administrative internships were listed, along with some of the ways in which you might be able to achieve these outcomes in your career development.

The internship is a unique form of learning. You control its success more directly than any other experience. Simply stated, you can gain as much as you wish by choices that you make about the ways in which you participate in your internship.

CHAPTER 3

Setting the Stage
for the Internship

Setting the stage for your internship requires you to engage in a number of interconnected but distinct activities. First, you should establish a set of goals for the internship experience. These goals will be influenced by several essential parameters, which include satisfying you university's degree requirements, continuing personal reflection on self-growth resulting from the experience, and meeting your sponsoring district's administrative and instructional needs. Second, you must gain support for your internship mission and goals. Third, you must design clear and articulate research proposals for your internship projects. Finally, you must establish a formal relationship with your sponsoring school district.

Establishing Internship Goals

An effective internship is one that is designed to achieve three major goals. First, it should provide you with an opportunity to experience leadership activities involving problem solving and decision making. This should give you a realistic understanding of how to apply theory to practice (university degree requirement). Second, by the time you have completed the experience you should have a clear and articulate understanding of whether or not you really want to be an educational leader. Your graduate classroom studies will help you understand the scope of the task educational leaders perform. Your internship will help you understand whether *you* like performing them (personal self-reflection). Finally, the internship should give you an opportunity to work on meaningful projects that will ultimately help your sponsoring school district develop and deliver better services to its students. This is the payback your district receives for sponsoring your internship (meeting school district's needs). It is easy to espouse these goals; achieving them is another matter. It will take careful planning and hard work.

At the outset, you should design an internship that concentrates on two types of leadership modes. First, you should seek to gain experience in the general practice of management. This will include such functions as running the general/central office, handling discipline problems, monitoring student attendance, developing budgets, dealing with parents, observing and evaluating teacher performance, and maintaining physical facilities, which are all part of an administrator's responsibilities. Second, you should seek to gain experience in the practice of leadership. This will include contemplating changes in the process and procedures that are used to meet student instructional needs, visioning the future of your district or building, practicing team problem solving and decision making, motivating staff to stay the course, and being a role model for faculty and staff.

In order for your internship to simulate these practices successfully, you must gain the support of and develop partnerships with a number of stakeholder groups. You must acquire the essential resources necessary to conduct and complete your work. You must also have the inner strength and willingness to do whatever it takes to do a good job. You *must* address these critical issues while you are planning your internship experience. Figure 3.1 defines some of the specific relationships and resources you will need to carry out a meaningful internship.

Establishing Relationships for a Meaningful Internship Experience

The success of your internship will depend, in part, on the types of partnerships you generate with appropriate stakeholder groups in your sponsoring school district. Remember that effective leadership depends on how leaders interact with a variety of individuals. Successful internships are similarly dependent. More often then not, interns need to work directly with many different people throughout the school district and/or within a school building. An important part of your internship responsibilities will be to convince these diverse stakeholder groups and their key representatives that their involvement in your projects is important to solving school district and/or building problems. Support for your internship must come from all quarters of the organizational spectrum.

Working With the Board of Education. Your internship experience should require the identification and solution of real administrative and instructional problems confronting your school district. In many instances, solving these

Figure 3.1. Relationships and Resources Necessary for a Meaningful Internship

---

Stakeholder Groups' Support and Partnership

The board of education should be apprised of your internship

Districtwide administration should know:

  The nature of your internship requirements and projects
  How they must facilitate your internship effort
  The impact of your internship work on the district

School building administration should know:

  The nature of your internship requirements and projects
  How they must facilitate your internship effort
  The impact of your internship work on the building

School building faculty (in all appropriate buildings) should know:

  What it means to be an administrative intern
  The nature of your internship projects
  Their role in the projects
  The impact of the projects on their work

School building support staff (in all appropriate buildings) should know:

  Their role in your projects
  The impact of your projects on their work

Acquisition of Essential Resources for the Successful Completion of an Internship

  The allocation of necessary funds to support your projects
  The purchase or identification of special equipment
  The purchase or identification of instructional material
  The identification of appropriate space

Inner Strength and Willingness to Do a Quality Job

  Possess the willingness to be a lifelong learner
  Possess the capability to be self-reflective
  Possess the desire to be a full-time practicing leader

---

problems will have a critical impact on student learning, organizational behavior, organizational culture, or organizational change. These problems and their corresponding solutions tend to be very complex and often involve the teaching staff as well as different administrative levels. In addition, they could require substantial financial support. In light of these circumstances, it is necessary for the board of education to be advised of your impending work. To begin with, you must have the board's assurance that it recognizes that the projects you are working on truly address real problems in the district. Consequently, the district's governing body should support any changes you propose or make. A solid partnership with the board of education could also help the credibility of your projects with the community at large. You will also need assurance that the board has or will be willing to provide financial support for your projects (if appropriate).

From the Field 3.1

It is not uncommon for a board of education to change its mind about how it wants to spend district money, even after it has been budgeted. It is very conceivable that you can begin your internship knowing that money has been allocated to support your work. Then as the year progresses, you may find that the board of education is forced to redirect some of its funds into a project that has nothing to do with your internship. You must understand that this is a reality that you will be confronted with every day of your practicing career. So, while presenting your internship plan to the board of education provides you with some assurance that it is aware of your existence and work, it should not be considered an indelible promise of board support.

Working With Districtwide Administration. One of the first partnerships you want to establish is with district administration. There are several good reasons for developing this partnership well in advance of the start of your internship. First, the superintendent of schools could function as a primary facilitator for your work. It is very possible that you will need an influential helping hand in cutting through red tape or opening political doors. The superintendent of schools would ordinarily be the one to perform such tasks. Consequently, getting the superintendent of schools on board early would be very advisable. Second, while you are planning your internship it is very important that you bring into balance what you must do to meet university requirements, what the district would like you to do to meet its needs, and what you personally would like to experience to help you determine if you want to pursue a career in educational leadership.

From the Field 3.2

Central administration often has a variety of projects on its agenda that require extra personnel. Interns are viewed as potential resources for such preset projects. You may have to balance your priorities and their wishes. You have to be careful to commit yourself to doing work that will enhance the achievement of your internship goals. On the other hand, you should be as facilitative as possible and re-spond positively to the wishes of your district leadership. Gaining a broad-based experience is important, but be careful not to overcommit yourself to tasks that have little or nothing to do with your internship responsibilities. Make sure that your district's central office leaders are in mutual agreement with your internship goals.

Furthermore, the work of the central administration in your school district could well be affected by your internship activities. For example, you could be responsible for designing a new districtwide policy to address student disci-pline. You might be asked to reform the way teacher performance is super-vised and evaluated. On the other hand, you might be experimenting with a peer mediation program in a school building, with the intent that the program would be turn-keyed in other district buildings. If your projects have the po-tential for districtwide influence, you should have the support of all district personnel who have professional responsibilities in related areas. These pro-jects, and your strategies for carrying them out, should be thoroughly dis-cussed with appropriate personnel prior to the start of your internship.

Finally, it is possible that the nature of your internship work would war-rant a field mentor who has districtwide responsibilities (e.g., an assistant su-perintendent for personnel, an assistant superintendent for instruction, or even the superintendent of schools, which often happens in smaller school districts). If this is so, it is only logical to discuss your internship experience at the district level early in the process.

Working With School Building Administration. Another partnership that should be developed beforehand is with building-level administration. Re-member, as a superintendent functions in the school district, so a principal functions in a school building. Thus, the reasons for early discussion at the building level parallel those at the district level. A principal can play the role of a primary facilitator in a building. It is very possible that you will need a special introduction to the faculty in your capacity as an administrative in-tern. The principal could make that introduction with a great degree of credi-bility. In addition, depending on the types of projects you are involved with, you may need similar introductions to students, parents, and any segment of the community serviced by the building. Once again, the principal should be the person who introduces you as an administrative intern to these groups.

From the Field 3.3

You must be very careful how you discuss your internship with your building prin-cipal. Past experience tells us that if principals are not self-confident or do not have a good sense of job security, they have a tendency to view interns as competition for their power base. Some principals are leery of sponsoring interns because they feel their staff may respond more positively to the intern's leadership than to their own leadership. In such situations, principals tend to use interns as behind-the-scenes workers. After the interns have developed whatever products are needed, these principals may present the work to their faculties as their own work. This deprives the interns of direct leadership experience, as well credit for their original work. This same behavior may be exhibited to inhibit intern contact or relationships with students, parents, and the community at large.

It is also important to discuss the design and focus of your internship projects with building administration. If you are going to do your internship in the building, some if not all of your projects should focus on building needs. Again, at the district level you should bring into balance what you must do to meet university requirements, what the building principal would like you to do, and what you personally would like to experience.

From the Field 3.4

You must be careful about how a principal asks you to use your time. There may be a tendency for the principal to assign you to multimanagement tasks (e.g., bus duty, calling parents about attendance, chaperoning after school events, covering lunchroom duty) that have little to do with leadership responsibilities. Experiencing these tasks is important, but they should not be your sole assignment during your internship. In some instances you may have already experienced these tasks as a classroom teacher. It is extremely important that the principal realizes what areas of leadership you must participate in to qualify for your degree. Once this information is clarified, you can be assigned appropriate types of tasks.

It is very possible that the work of the building's administration could be affected by your internship activities. Successful projects could have an effect on teacher duties and responsibilities, standards for student learning, or the strategies for dealing with parents and/or the community at large. If your project is going to have such influences on a building's organizational climate or culture, or the delivery of services to students, or how building personnel must relate to parents and the community, you should thoroughly discuss your project strategies and outcomes with appropriate personnel.

Finally, when an intern aspires to the position of principal, the building principal may act as the intern's field mentor. Consequently, it is logical to have the principal involved in the planning stages of your internship.

Working With School Faculty. If your internship is designed to provide you with an in-depth opportunity to experience leadership, you will need followers. As Ferdinand Drucker says very clearly, "The only definition of a leader is someone who has followers" (Hesselbein, Goldsmith, & Beckhard, 1996). This being the case, you will be working directly with school faculty during your internship, and you are going to have to convince them to participate in your projects. It is possible that many of the faculty have been your colleagues for some time, and that is where things can get a bit touchy. During your internship experience, you may be viewed as "neither fish nor fowl" by some of your fellow teachers. They may have difficulty putting your role in proper perspective. Some will view your work as preparation to "go over to the other side." Others will continue to treat you as a colleague who is complying with university requirements for a degree program.

What may make your relationship with faculty difficult will be the type of work in which you will be involved. If you are truly working on administrative tasks, you will have to play the role of a leader to some extent (within the confines of the law). At times you may be required to ask faculty to attend meetings after (or before) school hours. You may be given an opportunity to observe teachers (informally, of course) with whom you have been friends for some time. It is possible that you may come away from these observations with a negative opinion about a colleague's effectiveness in the classroom. There are innumerable possibilities that may alter your relationship with your colleagues during your internship.

This is why it is extremely important that you are introduced to the staff within your internship role. This introduction should clearly explain what you are going to do, how it relates to the staff role, what your authority base is (and is not), and how your success is dependent upon their participation and help. This introduction should take place at the beginning of the year (or just before you officially begin your internship). The faculty should have an opportunity to question you and the administration about the entire experience. They should be very clear about what you are doing and how it may affect them.

From the Field 3.5

Interns have reported two specific situations they have confronted when dealing with the teaching staff in a district or a building. Initially, these interns reported that their colleagues indicated they would help the interns in whatever way they could (this promise usually came well in advance of the beginning of the internship). They indicated a willingness to be on committees. They indicated a willingness to participate in experimentation that would require retraining and a change in teaching strategies. However, when it came time to attend the 3:30 p.m. meeting or to get involved in a new reading program experiment, few were willing to participate. This was especially true if it was a contract negotiation year.

Another common occurrence was that faculty asked interns to breach confidentiality and report on the details of an administrative decision. Interns also were approached to influence administration to make certain decisions in favor of faculty.

While the number of such incidents could be minimal, it should be understood that such requests could come without any warning. Interns must realize that they have *no* authority or influence, nor should they seek to attempt anything that might jeopardize their standing as an educational leader in training. As for staff who are suddenly unwilling to volunteer, neither the intern nor the field mentor can require their participation (unless it is contractual). On the other hand, if participation is mandatory, interns should seek help from field mentors and practicing administrators to make sure everyone is following their professional obligations.

Working With School Building Support Staff. In planning your internship you should make every effort to determine how much you will depend on support staff. All too often these individuals are totally forgotten during the planning stages of any project, and their presence and quality efforts are assumed to be available to the intern when they are needed for project help. It would not be in the best interest of anyone, including you, to make these assumptions. Secretaries, custodians, and maintenance staff have an extremely important role in the success of any type of activity or project. They deserve to receive the same early notification about your internship activities and expectations to ensure their support and quality services as does the superintendent of schools, principal, and members of the board. Keep in mind that administrators and board members will more than likely be guests at internship events, but support staff will be your daily co-workers.

To illustrate the need for early notification to support staff, imagine running a multiweek inservice for several hundred professional staff members. Now think of who is going to send notification letters to potential participants, register those who wish to take advantage of the inservice, and set up the meeting place so it is ready on demand. The answers to these questions should be clear.

You need to meet with the appropriate support staff in your sponsoring district and clarify how you will be depending on them during your internship.

Acquiring Essential Resources for Your Internship

The success of your internship will in part be dependent upon the quality and quantity of human, material, facility, and financial resources. During the planning stage of your internship, it is most imperative that you determine whether appropriate resources will be available and at your disposal for all of

Figure 3.2. Types of Resources Used During Internships

Human Resources

Have faculty members been identified as special project participants?

Have faculty members been identified as committee members?

Has support staff been identified for all projects and activities?

Have outside consultants been considered?

Material Resources

Have all instructional programs been purchased?

Has all instructional equipment been purchased?

Has all inservice equipment been purchased or reserved?

Has all audio-visual equipment been purchased or reserved?

Facility Resources

Has all required space been identified and reserved?

Has all space been appropriately remodeled?

Financial Resources

Has the board of education released funds for project costs?

Has the board of education earmarked funds for future purchases?

Has the board of education approved stipends for faculty participation?

Has the board of education approved the purchase of material resources?

Has the board of education approved funds for facility costs?

---

your internship activities. Be very careful to reconsider any project recommendations that will depend on anticipated resources. Figure 3.2 suggests some questions about resources that you should answer.

All necessary resources should be on hand before you attempt to undertake any internship activities. If you are pressed into participating in any activities that do not have available resources, it is important to identify this fact at the beginning of your internship. It is also recommended that you have a contingency "plan B" in case the resources do not arrive in time. The situation of not receiving essential resources in time to conduct a project is a common occurrence in the real world of leadership practice. If this happens during your internship, you will have experienced one of the inevitable improvisations made by full-time practicing school administrators. You should not think of an event like this as a failure. Think of it as an opportunity to reform the project and continue on.

From the Field 3.6

Interns have sometimes found themselves without appropriate resources at critical junctures in their projects. In some cases, boards of education made last minute decisions not to purchase equipment, software, or instructional material that was necessary for project goal achievement. In other cases, staff positions were not filled in time to provide all the help necessary to meet project objectives. It is important that you obtain all the necessary commitments from your district administration to acquire the resources you need to conduct your internship project, but have a contingency plan in mind just in case these commitments fall through.

Remember that it is important to discuss the acquisition of resources with the board of education and district administration well in advance of the beginning of your internship.

Do You Really Want to Be a School Administrator?

Your internship should be designed to provide you with a real-life experience of educational leadership. It should challenge your inner strength to answer the question, "Do I really want to be an educational leader?" You must be honest and realistic with yourself. Up to now, you have been in the classroom studying the knowledge and skills successful educational leaders need to possess. To the best of your ability, you have acquired that knowledge and those skills; now you must go into a real-life situation and use them. The internship should not be designed to protect you from real-life situations. It should help open your eyes to the daily leadership problems and situations that you have often heard about but never believed. Finding yourself in such situations may cause you to question your leadership ability, your logic, and even your basic common sense. But all this is necessary if you are to have a meaningful experience. Just remember that an internship should not be designed to be purposefully "difficult," it should be purposefully "real."

From the Field 3.7

Be prepared to experience situations that will challenge your activity time lines, intended outcomes, and available resources. Interns in the past have been amazed at colleagues who are unwilling to meet after school and individuals who openly exhibit "I-don't-care" attitudes even when successful projects could mean better student performance. Experience also tells us that boards of education have reneged on their promises to purchase materials that are needed to support internship activities. However, these things do happen, and as an educational leader you have to be prepared to handle them with quality knowledge and skills.

You will have to exhibit a great degree of patience throughout your internship experience. It will be a unique opportunity to learn how school administrators must function in the real world. You must be a lifelong learner. You should not assume that you know everything. You should seek to learn from every experience and catalog it for future reference. Your internship will help you be a successful school administrator in the future. You have to like people and like dealing with people all day, every day. You must be flexible and willing to amend your agenda to meet the unexpected as well as the ebb and flow of daily activity in a school building. You will not be "in control"; you will be a leader.

The Internship Project Proposal

Identifying Internship Projects and Activities

Internship projects and activities are made up of a combination of three factors. First, the university will require that you complete a number of specific assignments to prove your ability to carry theory to practice. The nature of these assignments is a matter of individual institutional preference. However, you will almost always have to satisfy an hourly requirement for work in different areas. For example, you may have to spend 100 hours of your internship working in a central office to learn how to manage a school building. Or, you may have to spend 200 hours involved in leading faculty on instructional projects, policy analysis exercises, or designing a new reading program.

In addition to satisfying time requirements, you may have to participate in specific types of activities that address current issues in the education profession. In some situations, universities may supply you with a list of generic problem areas, and you will have to decide what specific problem you wish to address (see Figure 3.3). In other situations, you may be given specific problems for which you must find a solution during the course of your internship.

Second, your sponsoring school district will want to take advantage of your internship and have you address some specific areas that are of concern to them. These problem areas could be issues that the district would have to address whether you were an intern there or not, but given your availability the district decides that your involvement will be less costly and time-consuming than using full-time practicing administrators. If these problems can be legitimized to meet university assignments and time requirements, you will have a perfect match. If not, you will have to make a decision as to whether you should or should not undertake the requested task. If it is a critical issue

Figure 3.3. General Problem Areas Related to Internship Projects

Problem Area*	Focus Points*
Risk management	Student discipline
	Special education
	Gifted education
	Personnel problems
Evaluation	Staff performance
	Instructional programs
Communication	Media
	Community
	Parents
	Staff
Technology/Administrative Procedures	Classroom management
	Instructional planning
	Instructional support
Change	Instructional programming
	Restructuring
	Reforming leadership styles
	Innovative scheduling
Diversity	Gender
	Race
	Multiculturalism

NOTE: * An intern in educational leadership would use these problem areas and focal points to develop related leadership projects.

that requires immediate attention, and it is directly related to student learning or safety, you might find yourself working overtime. Don't worry—this is real-life administration. It is highly recommended that you try to interrelate your university requirements with your sponsoring school district's needs.

Third, there will be certain types of problems, issues, and activities that you will want to experience. It may be that you have researched an approach to student discipline and would like to test it in a realistic situation. Once again, if you can match your own desires to the needs of the school district and the requirements of the university, you will have a perfect match. If not, you may have to conduct your experiment outside the parameters of your internship, or you may have to wait and try your ideas at some other time.

The first step to problem identification is to find out what university requirements you must satisfy for your degree conferment. The second step is to approach your sponsoring school district for a conversation with either the district administration or the school building administration. How you determine which one to visit first is dictated by the focus of your internship and the potential location of your field mentor. Consequently, an internship for a principal's certification would warrant an initial discussion with building administration, while an internship for a district administrator's position would warrant an initial discussion with the superintendent.

Wherever the conversation begins, it should focus on your degree requirements vis-à-vis school building needs. The first question you want to answer is, "How can I satisfy my university requirements, while helping the school building address some critical issues related to helping students learn better?" A second question to be answered is, "How will addressing these needs provide me with an opportunity to enhance and extend my own leadership skills?" Answering these questions should give you valuable data to help determine the focus of your internship experience. You will have specified the projects that you will be responsible for during the internship experience. You will also be able to advise university personnel as to how your district will facilitate your internship. Finally, by answering these questions you will be prepared to start planning your internship.

Are you aware of the types of problems that might currently exist in your school district and that might be logical for you to focus on as potential internship projects? List specific problem situations in your school district that would relate to the problems areas identified.

Problem Area	*District Problem Situation*
Risk Management	_____
	_____
	_____
Evaluation	_____
	_____
	_____
Communication	_____
	_____
	_____

Technology   _____

               _____

               _____

Change   _____

               _____

               _____

               _____

Diversity   _____

               _____

               _____

               _____

The Internship Project Proposal Design

A successful internship is not based on "luck." As the old saying goes, "Luck is the residue of good planning." For your internship, "planning" and "project proposal" mean the same thing. If you have well-thought-out, articulately written project proposals, you will help ensure the success of your internship.

Before you begin writing project proposals it is important to investigate their potential for success. This can be accomplished by answering a set of questions, as illustrated in Figure 3.4. These questions can be used in your initial discussions with districtwide and building-level administration. If it is convenient, you will want to ask the same questions of faculty and staff who would be involved in your projects.

Your project(s) will be complex undertakings. They will require input from a number of staff members from all levels of the organizational spectrum. You will need to develop a great deal of faith in how others conduct themselves in the work place. Good leaders not only know how to delegate responsibilities, they also know how to give workers their own space to do their jobs. However, that does not mean that leaders do not check up to make sure everything is going according to plan. During your internship you should do the same. Remember, you do not have much room for error. You have to complete your internship experience within a preset time limit. So, make sure that all staff meet their job responsibilities for your project(s).

Figure 3.4. Proposal Development Questions

Before you begin to plan and design an internship project, try to obtain answers to the following questions:

1. Is the project manageable?

   a. Do I have enough time to complete the project?

   b. Are all project resources available?

   c. Have all appropriate staff been identified and notified?

2. Does the project focus on a problem area that will be supported by those who will eventually be affected by its solution?

   a. Do all stakeholder groups support the need for the project?

   b. Will all stakeholder groups have a sustained interest in the project?

   c. Is it necessary to check with potential participants about their interest in the project before committing to do the work?

3. Does the project solution have the potential to make a contribution to its intended goal(s)?

   a. Is the project significant to the missions of the district, building, department, or grade level?

   b. What problems might be created by the solution to the problems under study?

   c. Are there any political and/or ethical concerns about the solution to this problem?

From the Field 3.8

Sometimes you can be denied necessary resources for reasons other than a lack of support from the board of education, administration, or faculty. An intern voiced frustration when a new instructional program that was a major role player in a project did not arrive on time. In fact, it arrived so late the project had to be aborted. The reason for the delay in the arrival of the instructional program was a clerical error made in the purchase order.

You must also be concerned about the amount of time it will take to begin and finish a project. You need to devise detailed time lines to determine if the project(s) can be completed within your internship. If it cannot, you must decide whether you can begin the project (and satisfy some internship requirements) and let the district complete the project post-internship, or if it would it be better not to include the project on your internship task list.

From the Field 3.9

Many interns find themselves agreeing to evaluate some type of instructional program (most often in the areas of reading, math, or language arts). Their intent is to assess whether student abilities in a given area increase or decrease through the use of the program. However, one of the primary sources of data to determine skill outcomes is year-end testing. What interns find is that test results often do not come back to the school district until mid to late June (if not later). This is typically long after their internships are over. Consequently, this type project cannot be completed.

Another area of concern is stakeholder support for the project itself. You must determine if teachers, support staff, and any appropriate stakeholder group (e.g., parents, the board of education) are behind the concept of the project. Do they really feel there is a problem that needs to be solved? Do they perceive the problem in a similar manner as you and/or the administration? Are they prepared to play a role in the implementation of a solution to the problem? Will they be there for the long haul? If you do not receive affirmative answers to such questions, your internship work may create a major problem rather than solve one. There should be mutual agreement by a majority of all stakeholder groups that a problem exists and should be solved. There should also be agreement that your strategy for solving the problem is viable and can be completed. There should be agreement on the cost of your strategy from all appropriate district stakeholder groups. These agreements should ensure the sustained interest of all role players from the beginning to the end of the project.

Finally, you should measure a project's intended outcome against the mission of the affected organizational unit. After all, if the project does not increase student learning or enhance efficiency of the delivery of services to students, you should question whether or not it should take up the district's valuable time and resources. Your project design should consider whether the solution will create additional and/or more severe problems once it is in place. You should also determine whether there are any political or ethical inconsistencies that must be addressed. Many times these issues appear if there is pressure from outside groups or the board of education to solve a problem in accordance with their own private agenda. For example, a group of parents might be dissatisfied with the way a bus route has been established. They may address this "problem" with a board member, who (in public, of course) may call for a reorganization of all district bus routes. The administration may then decide that this would be a good exercise for an administrative intern. Consequently, you find it on your agenda. More often than not, committing yourself to this type of project could have a more deleterious effect on your psyche than on the district's ability to provide bus service to its students.

Once you have determined that a project would be a viable undertaking, it is time to think about how to organize it for implementation. The organization of a project should be applied to a specific proposal design. You must remember that you will most likely have to present the project idea to different groups at different times. Thus you should organize your presentation and project description in a consistent manner. A proposal design will provide you with that consistency.

There are many different configurations for such proposal designs; however, they usually all contain very similar elements. Your proposal design should seek to answer two major questions. First, "What is to be learned from the implementation of this project?" Second, "How will the project be implemented?" Figure 3.5 lists the questions and subquestions that should be addressed during the proposal design stage.

- What is to be learned from the implementation of your project?

The first question embraces the conceptual component of your project proposal. It focuses attention on specific questions that you must answer to achieve the project's intended purpose. It defines the applicability of the project solution beyond the borders of its setting. For example, if you were experimenting with a specific program, in a specific building, at a specific grade level, but wanted to expand the program to other buildings and/or grade levels, this is where you would explain those intentions.

From the Field 3.10

Whenever project proposals are presented, they should be supported by theory. One of the major criticisms of practicing educational leaders focuses on their inability to put theory into practice. It is most logical to interweave any data from current and major studies that will support the foci of the project. It is also logical to include major studies that support an opposite point of view and show how your project intends to refute such views.

Defining the Project Problem. Your project problems could emanate from a vast number of sources and be suggested by districtwide, building, department, grade-level, and personnel experiences. They could rise out of professional reading, a previous course project, or a particular regulation passed by

Figure 3.5. Questions for the Development of a Project Proposal*

What is to be learned from the implementation of your project?

1. What is the topic of this project?
2. What is the specific intent(s) of this project?
3. Why is this project important?
4. What are the major questions and subquestions to be answered by this project?
5. What are the limitations of this project?

What methodology will be used for the implementation of your project?

1. Where will the project take place?
2. What population will be used for the project?
3. What instrumentation will be used for data gathering?
4. How will the project data be analyzed?
5. What specific tasks are to be used in the implementation of the project?

NOTE: * Not all projects will require that all questions be answered.

the state legislature that requires school districts to effect some change. Whatever its source, every project problem needs to be clearly and articulately defined.

Remember, if you are going to build a followership that will participate in your project, you must have a convincing argument that the project will help children learn better, school buildings run better, or teachers teach better. Formulate your argument by answering the question, "What is the topic of this project?" A clear, concise answer to this question will achieve several things. First, it will help to develop a theoretical framework to guide you in the implementation of your work. Second, it will provide you with an opportunity to set the project in some historical perspective. Third, it will help you focus on the specific questions that you should be addressing as you go along in your work. Fourth, it will help you present a strong rationale for the conduct of the project. Finally, it will help you place the project focus in current research and literature.

From the Field 3.11

This exercise of topic definition may seem far removed from practical use. When practicing administrators are questioned as to why they don't use processes like this, they claim they don't have the time. Some may even say other administration, staff or the board of education would not appreciate their work. Keep in mind that these are excuses not to do the work. Here are some reasons why you should always practice this step:

1. Do it for your own professional growth.

2. It will provide project supporters with information to help convert disbelievers.

3. It should be done to help everyone know how decisions are made to spend taxpayer money so children can learn better.

It is important that you begin your proposal with a high degree of clarity. Booth, Colomb, and Williams (1995) suggest a three-step process to achieve this goal.

1. Complete the sentence, "I want to learn about _____."

2. Expand this sentence to answer the questions, "who, what, where, when, whether, and/or how."

3. Answer the questions, "contribute to how/why/what."

An illustration of how this three-step process might appear is the following statement:

> I want to learn about the organizational and instructional efficiency of block scheduling on the delivery of instructional services to high school students in order to determine if the high school should use this scheduling formula beginning in the 2000-2001 school year.

Now it is your turn to use Booth, Colomb, and Williams's suggestion as it would apply to one of your internship projects. Write a statement using the three-step process that defines your project.

_____

_____

_____

Identifying the Specific Intent of a Project. This section of your proposal should define the central concept of the project. It is important to articulate clearly the core of the project's purpose. If you do not clearly state the purpose of the project, you will have difficulty implementing a strategy to solve whatever problem is at hand. You will also have difficulty getting others to understand what it is you wish them to accomplish. This could affect their desire and their enthusiasm to participate in the project.

Creswell (1998) provides a "script" to improve your presentation of the central theory of your project. This script requires four specific applications:

1. Identify a "specific tradition of inquiry." This relates to the specific type of inquiry approach that you will use to collect and analyze data, as well as to write the final project report.

2. Specify "words that indicate the action of the [intern] and the focus of the tradition." For example, *understand* is best related to biographical studies, *describe* is best related to case studies and ethnographies. You also *develop* or *generate* grounded theory. However, you can *discover* in any inquiry genre.

3. Define the unit of analysis to be used in the project. This relates to individuals, groups, processes, and so on.

4. Define the central focus of the project.

The Creswell script reads as follows:

The purpose of this *(indicate the type of tradition of inquiry to be used in the project)* study is to *(indicate an action word)* the *(indicate the central focus of the project)* for *(indicate the unit of analysis)*. At this stage in the [project], the *(restate the central focus of the project)* will be generally defined as *(give a general definition of the central concept)*.

The following is an illustration of a statement of purpose using the Creswell script.

The purpose of this study is to describe the advantages and disadvantages of block scheduling on the delivery of instructional services to high school students. This study will result in a feasibility report to inform teachers, administrators, board members, students, and parents of its findings and conclusions. The use of a block scheduling formula for the high school means providing students and teachers with an opportunity to interact innovatively and creatively in the learning process while using time-on-task in an efficient manner.

Now it's your turn. Using the Creswell script write a statement of purpose for one of your internship projects. To maintain continuity, try to use the same project that you cited in the exercise on defining the project problem.

_____

_____

_____

_____

_____

_____

Defining the Importance of Your Project. By and large, as a school adminis-trator you will find yourself functioning as a salesperson. A very important part of your project proposal has to do with defining the significance of the work. You are answering such questions as, "Why should we undertake the project?" and "How will the students (district, building) benefit from the ef-fort?" You must be very convincing. A clearly spelled out statement of signifi-cance will provide project supporters and participants with data to justify their feelings and participation. It will also give them information to convince skeptics and detractors.

This section should seek to answer such questions as the following:

1. How does this project positively enhance district services to students?
2. How does this project positively enhance a district (building) adminis-trative process?
3. How does this project positively enhance student achievement?
4. How does this project positively impact the cost-effective use of tax-payers' dollars?
5. How does this project positively impact teachers' instructional deliv-ery systems?
6. How does this project positively enhance the district's (building's) im-age with the public?

Think of one of your internship projects. How does it positively enhance or impact:

District services to students

_____

_____

A districtwide administrative process

_____

_____

Student achievement

_____

_____

Cost-effective use of taxpayers' dollars

_____

_____

Teachers' instructional delivery systems

_____

_____

District (building) image with the public

_____

_____

Other significant reasons why the project should be implemented

_____

_____

_____

Defining the Questions Your Project Will Answer. Now that you have identified the topic, intent, and significance of your project, you need to develop guidelines for an implementation strategy. You can begin this by asking what major *questions* the project seeks to answer. This will help to demarcate the project. In effect, this sets the project boundaries. You may find you need to develop only two or three major project questions. However, listing related subquestions will further refine each major question. Here are some project questions for the illustration we have been using throughout this section.

1. What are the perceptions of administrators, faculty, and students regarding using a block scheduling formula?
   a. What are the perceptions of building administrators regarding the instructional advantages of block scheduling?
   b. What are the perceptions of teaching faculty regarding the instructional advantages of block scheduling?
   c. What are the perceptions of students regarding the instructional advantages of block scheduling?

2. Can block scheduling be implemented in the high school without violating any compliance regulation that must be adhered to?

   a. Will the teachers' contract be violated by the implementation of a block schedule?
   b. Will any board of education policies be violated by the implementation of a block schedule?
   c. Will any state statutes be violated by the implementation of a block schedule?

Describing the Limitations of Your Project. It is important that you place boundaries on your project. To begin with, your internship lasts for a specific duration of time. Usually, this time is a maximum of one academic year. You will find that no matter how much of an academic year you have, it will not be enough to complete all aspects of your project. Consequently, it is good to think of working on a smaller scale with small groups, such as a grade level or a department or perhaps a building, to experiment with an idea, rather than with the entire district. If the project works, it can be turn-keyed for a larger group. You can also limit a project by using some unique aspect(s) of a group. This would result in your selecting a sample of a larger group. On the other hand, the unique aspects of your project might naturally limit its boundaries. For example, it might be related to a specific group of special needs students or to an administrative process that can be used only in the district's central office.

Limiting the size and parameters of your project will

1. Create a manageable undertaking (time-wise, material-wise, and cost-wise)

2. Provide you with an opportunity to observe the unique phenomenon of your idea in a closed, controlled environment

3. Give you the opportunity to make reasonable recommendations to carry the project forward or to dissolve it, without creating a major cost to the board of education

4. Keep the level of emotionality regarding change down in the building

5. Implement the change process at a reasonable pace

- What methodology will be used for the implementation of your project?

The second set of questions that you must address in the development of a project proposal has to do with its design and methodology. These questions relate to describing the specific population that will be involved in the project, how you will collect data, how you will analyze the data, and the specific tasks that you will employ to conduct the project.

Describing the Site and/or Population of Your Project. You must be very mindful of who the subjects of your work will be and where they reside. Very often your subjects will possess unique characteristics that will dictate how you approach the project. This also holds true for where the subjects are located. For example, you could be doing a project with gifted students who are in a self-contained learning environment that houses special instructional equipment to meet their unique needs. The group of (gifted) students could possess unique abilities that are not ordinarily found in regular mainstream classes. The instructional equipment could be unique to the students' abilities (e.g., specially programmed computers).

A clear description of the project population and site will help in expressing findings to colleagues and other stakeholders, give balance to recommendations, reduce the potential for misinterpretation of findings, provide a clear understanding of who can be helped by receiving similar services, and provide a clear springboard for proper turn-keying activities.

From the Field 3.12

Choosing a site or a sample population may not be within your authority. It is very possible that the project problem(s) are already located by virtue of their contextual nature (e.g., one cannot relocate the evaluation of a districtwide eighth-grade math program). However, there might be a time when you will have a choice. If so, here are some tips regarding the selection of a particular site or population sample.

1. You should be able to work with a group of faculty without carrying too much baggage. If the faculty knows you well, that does not necessarily mean they will be more helpful. Sometimes familiarity breeds "not on your life will I stay after school for your meetings." Choose co-participants who have a stake in the outcome of the project. Try to foster good strong partnerships with participants. Play the role of an effective leader.

2. Make sure that someone in authority has properly briefed co-participants on the importance of the work to be done. It is not good for someone to address this group and say, "We are doing this because so-and-so is an administrative intern." It would be better if they said, "This is a project that must be completed if we are going to provide you with resources that will help our eighth-grade students score better on the state math exam. So-and-so, who is an administrative intern this year, will be chairing the committee. Good luck on a successful project." The second introduction places the project in proper perspective. It also conveys the message that the project would have been done even if you were not an administrative intern.

3. Try to stay away from any settings where there are political or ethical complications (real or impending). Remember, you are an individual with ad-

ministrative aspirations, not a crusader who will make things better in the building for all time.

Former interns have indicated that their experiences tested their patience in ways they never thought possible. That's good, because as a practicing administrator you will have the opportunity to experience this feeling many times over.

Describing Your Data Gathering Procedures. Data gathering is a complex process that will in large part determine the success of your project. Do not take these procedures lightly. Remember you are conducting your project *in the real world*. Most likely you will not have a second chance to gather the necessary data to complete your project. You must think clearly about which research genre you are going to use (qualitative or quantitative), as well as which tradition you are going to employ (biography, phenomenology, grounded theory, ethnography, case study, etc.). A specific type of data gathering technique best serves each research genre and tradition. You must carefully research the techniques that will provide you with the information you need to properly complete your project.

Creswell (1998) envisions data gathering as a series of interrelated steps that includes activities that go beyond data gathering. What is extremely interesting about Creswell's approach, and very important to you as an administrative intern, is the importance he places on activities that might not be thought of under normal circumstances as crucial to the process. Figure 3.6 illustrates the steps in the Creswell data collection circle and also relates them to a project setting.

From the Field 3.13

Many of you will be doing your internship in the district where you teach. At first glance, this will seem to be most advantageous. After all, you know the staff very well, and they know you. In all probability, you have served on committees with those who are not members in your department or don't teach in your school building. Another enticing fact is that your field mentor could well be an administrator who helped hire you into the district. Also, the students will know you as a teacher. If you have good rapport with them, you might feel that they will be of more help than hindrance. There is a certain degree of comfort that you will gain from such a situation.

Interns from the past have reported that all is not grand and glorious in such situations. To begin with, now that you are an administrative intern, members of the teaching staff and the students will have to view you from the "other side of the desk." If you must still teach your assignment during the internship, this will

(continued on page 52)

Figure 3.6. Adaptation of Creswell's Data Collection Circle to a Project Setting

---

Locating Site and Subjects: You must find the right participants in the right setting.

If you are implementing an experimental districtwide instructional program, you must carefully choose buildings, teachers, and classes that will be involved in the project. You want to find willing participants who will not compromise the experiment so you will be able to collect good information that can be used in turn-key activities.

Gaining Access to the Site and Subjects: You must enter the site location and the "turf" of the participants with proper introductions, so they know what you are up to, how you expect to go about your work, and what you expect of them during the implementation of the project.

You must be careful that you touch all the appropriate bases before you begin a project. You may need to present your project proposal to the board of education, building administration, and faculty. There may be need for you to present information to students. If you are going to include students in some type of data gathering technique, there may be a need for you to have parental permission.

Determining a Sample Population: You must have a clear and articulate understanding of who should be part of the project. You will need to establish specific criteria that can be used for selecting who should be part of your project.

You should make certain that the sample population of your project possesses all of the appropriate characteristics necessary for full participation. If you are implementing an experimental instructional program, you should make sure that all students have been exposed to the program material in the way it was designed. You have to make sure that teachers did not deviate from the project guidelines or were unable to complete all assignments in the required amount to time.

Collecting Project Data: You must be sure that you choose the appropriate data collecting approaches for your project. In many instances, the type of research tradition you use will dictate the type of data collection procedure you need to employ.

In the implementation of an experimental instructional program, you will be interested in gathering student achievement data (specialized and/or standardized test). You will be interested in students' attitudes toward the program (interview and/or classroom observation). You will also be interested in the teachers' attitudes toward the program's ability to expose students to ap-

Figure 3.6. Continued

propriate information, the facility of instructional delivery, perhaps a comparison to other programs (interview and/or survey). You will want to obtain building- and department-level administrators' attitudes toward the program (interview and/or survey).

Recording Project Data: You must code and record data in a consistent, simple way.

Regardless of the types of protocols you use, make sure all information is reported in a way that lets you easily see the relationships you are looking for in the data. If you are measuring student achievement, you need to make sure the same test protocols are being used for all student participants. If you are interviewing teachers and administrators, make sure the interview schedules are tailored to each role function. You should develop them in such a way that they permit you to place all collected data in convenient places. Make sure your protocols are as simple as possible.

Handling Issues That Arise in the Field: You must be prepared for any and all uncharted situations that can arise during the implementation of your project.

The fact that you are implementing a project in the "real world" means that it will be subject to all of the nuances of that world. Remember your proposal is a predesigned plan that is subject to change at the demand of the environment within which it is to take place. So, such occurrences as unannounced strikes, board decisions to spend money differently, teacher unwillingness to participate fully, lack of parental support, or community disapproval will certainly cause you to make midcourse corrections. These actions and attitudes could cause you to change data collection instrumentation, project participants, or even project goals.

Data Storage: You must predetermine the strategies you want to use for storing data.

If you are handling a large amount of data, you should design schemes for coding and storing information before the project begins. You should not let data collect (the "I'll get to it over the Christmas break" syndrome). Data can become stale if you don't attend to them on a routine basis. This is especially true when using interview and observation protocols. Many times, while using these protocols, you will observe or hear something that you cannot record immediately but that should be defined as soon as the interview or observation session is over. Remember, we are not saying to analyze the data, just store it properly so it can be analyzed at an appropriate time.

increase their confusion about your role. In addition, teachers and students might not be in agreement with some of your decisions. There may also be attempts to compromise your project data. Some interns have reported that colleagues pressured them to change report conclusions and modify recommendations even though project data did not support such modifications.

These illustrations do not cover a majority of the internships that we have sponsored. They are just a tip that you should keep in the back of your mind. If any of these things happen, you should report them to your field mentor right away.

When you are developing the instrumentation that you plan to use during data collection activities, you should be aware of several things:

1. Keep the design of the protocol as simple as possible. Complex designs can confuse respondents.

2. Be very clear in your instructions. If respondents do not understand what they are supposed to do, they may answer the protocol incorrectly.

3. Provide respondents with an opportunity to voluntarily opt out of the exercise.

4. Make sure you provide all protection the respondent might need to make a meaningful contribution to the project (such as providing confidentiality or anonymity to respondents, if necessary).

5. Make sure that wherever possible your protocols include an opportunity for respondents to identify themselves voluntarily.

Analyzing Project Data. This section of your proposal should address the answers to two questions. One question is, "How will meaning be brought to the collected project data?" A second question is, "How will the data be presented to the audience for which the project is intended?" Rossman and Rallis (1998) suggest six procedures for typical generic data analysis. By adding this information to your proposal, you would be describing how you would conduct the data analysis for your project.

1. Develop a data inventory on note cards. Explain how you intend to inventory data collected through the use of specially designed protocols, and how you will use any anecdotal data that you may accumulate along the way.

2. Become familiar with the data. Explain the approach you intend to use to become familiar with your project data. You should not look for shortcuts when you are doing this. The more familiar you are with the data, the better they will serve you as you begin your analysis. You must become intimate with all appropriate project data.

3. Develop themes, categories, and patterns for your data. Describe how you will organize the data so you can become familiar with them and assess them in terms of their relationship to your major project questions.

4. Coding data. Explain how you will code the data once you have related them to your broader themes. You need to design ways to determine what data related to these broad based areas are truly essential to your project outcomes.

5. Identifying alternative understandings about your data. Explain how you are going to look for diversified explanations that may be elicited by your project data. You cannot always accept the obvious. You must indicate how you intend to challenge the obvious.

6. Identifying how you intend to write the final report. Describe what your final report will look like and how it will proceed to help its intended audience. Much of the shaping of a final report can be accomplished during data analysis. In this section you should decide whether the report will be a formal paper, a monograph, a handbook, or any number of other publication presentations. This explanation should be accompanied by a rationale as to why you have chosen that particular format.

Developing a Task List for Project Implementation. Now that you have put together a winning proposal, it is time to take a step back. Think through all the different types of activities that you will have to engage in to implement the project successfully. Your goal here is to put together a comprehensive task list. There are a number of generic thought patterns that you should complete for every project in your internship.

1. Think about all of the individuals and groups that you must meet with during the project. Put them on a list.

2. Think about all of the activities that you must engage in with each individual and/or group.

3. Think about all the activities that you must conduct yourself.

4. List the activities and their respective groups or individuals on a time line that stretches from the projected beginning date to the projected completion date.

From the Field 3.14

Past experience has shown that interns tend to forget several critical activity groups when they are developing their project task lists. They also forget to conduct follow-up meetings with decision-making personnel. When you are developing a task list, it is better to overload the list. As you implement the project you can make decisions as to whether or not a task is necessary.

Do not forget to list research activities that are critical to the project's success. Spending time in the library researching a project is a legitimate task. Also, remember to build in benchmarks for reporting back to your field mentor and/or central office administration to get midcourse corrections. While it is good to build in these meetings when you are developing the project proposal, it is possible that these administrators will decide that it is not necessary to meet with you. Remember to let them make that decision. Also remember that not meeting with these people can be as much of a problem as having to meet with them all the time.

Conducting a Literature Review

One of the more important inclusions in your project proposal is a literature review on the focus of your project. The importance of this exercise cannot be overestimated. One of the most critical complaints about practicing administrators is their inability or lack of desire to translate theory into practice. In surveys conducted across the nation, principals report that the percentage of time they spend reading current literature is very low. When literature reviews are assigned in graduate classes, a wince of anguished pain is prominently displayed on the faces of a majority of students.

The fact is, a good literature review will give credence to the intended goals of a project. It will provide important information about the research content of the project, as well as a support rationale for the significance of the project. Finally, it will influence your project design, instrumentation for data collection, and data analysis plan.

Literature reviews are most often stand-alone sections of project proposals. Our suggestion is to deviate from the norm and interweave literature research into three different sections of your proposal. Include it in the project problem definition section. This will help to ground the definition of the problem in theory, as well as provide support for the validity of the problem. The second place it belongs is the section on the purpose of the project. Research literature will help establish the intent of the project and ground it in theory. The third section that benefits from a literature review is the one on the significance of the project. Research literature could help support the importance of the project and achieving its intended outcomes.

Changing the Proposal During Implementation. Your project proposal is a guideline for implementation. It was developed in a pure environment. If you are a careful planner, you probably have accounted for different types of unique experiences that might occur in your school district that could affect the outcome of the project. However, there are many forces at work in the complex organization of a school district that could have an effect on the project. It is impossible to predict them all. You are going to have to deal with uncharted events that will cause you to modify your project plan. This phenomenon is not unusual. You must handle it with a professional attitude and do the best you can to hold the project intact to achieve your original intent. Make sure you understand that your project proposal must be flexible. Field issues will continue to have effects on your plan.

Developing a Formal Internship Agreement With the School District

The final phase of setting the stage for your internship is the relationship that connects you with your university program and your sponsoring school district. Your internship will require you to spend many hours over and above your normal workday. In most instances, school districts do not give interns time off so they can conduct their projects. In addition, many universities do not negotiate with school districts to give interns release time for internship responsibilities. In addition to working two full-time jobs, you will be accepting the responsibility to be productive and to complete numerous exercises that will challenge your leadership skills.

Your sponsoring school district will expect you to perform in a productive manner. You will be responsible for helping the district address real problems that must be resolved in order to improve services to students.

Your university will also play an important role in your internship by expecting your leadership skills to be challenged, honed, and advanced. Ultimately, it will determine if you are ready to receive your degree and be certified as a practicing administrator.

These are complex relationships. They require specific guidelines for all parties concerned. Consequently, it is necessary to have a formal agreement that specifies the ground rules by which all parties must abide during the internship practice. The following discussion focuses on the terms of a formal administrative internship working agreement.

Conditions of Internship

To participate in an internship you should be enrolled in a qualified master of arts or doctoral program in school administration (educational leadership). There are several conditions that are generic to any internship. First, you are fully responsible for being aware of the university requirements you must meet in order to complete your degree work successfully. Your sponsoring school district does not have any responsibility to remind you of these requirements. In addition, your sponsoring school district has no obligation to provide you with release time or financial rewards for work over and above your normal duties and responsibilities.

From the Field 3.15

There are some programs that require that you take time off from your regular job and serve as a full-time administrative intern. These types of programs are disappearing as time goes on. They are not thought of as "user friendly." However, some interns have reported that they have been given time off by their own school district to complete their studies. This may happen because of district policy or because of a union contract agreement. In some districts you may be forgiven study hall or lunchroom duty. You may even be released from bus duty. These are the normal release time benefits afforded interns. Under normal circumstances you are required to complete your internship without the benefit of any release time from your teaching duties and responsibilities.

Supervision of the Intern

The agreement should indicate that your field mentor is your primary supervisor. If you have an opportunity to choose this person, you should seek an individual who will be able to open doors, cut through red tape, and provide you with credible introductions around the district. You should also look for an individual who knows and understands the culture of the school district. Even though you have been a teacher in the district, you will now be viewing the culture (and vice versa) from an administrative perspective. In addition to your field mentor, the agreement should indicate that your university mentor is responsible for observing you in leadership activities. It should also accord both mentors the responsibility for making suggestions for midcourse corrections and advising you as to how you are to handle field issues.

Reports and Thesis/Dissertation

There should be a clause in the working agreement that clearly spells out what written work you are responsible for producing during your internship. This clause should spell out the specific reports or formal research paper(s) on your work that you must generate. The clause is a protection for you in that the sponsoring school district will know exactly what you must accomplish. The school district should work in conjunction with the university to make sure you are exposed to a significant amount of work, but within the limitations of your requirements.

Intern Evaluation

The document should state who is responsible for your evaluation. Obviously, both mentors will have responsibilities in this area. However, there should be a clear indication as to who the primary evaluator will be and what relationship the other mentor has to the evaluation process. There should be benchmarks identifying when formative and summative evaluations are due. There should also be one or more evaluation protocols to be completed by the responsible parties.

Internship Follow-Up

Internship programs are systems that can always be designed to be more efficient and effective. Therefore the work agreement should call for a debriefing session with the intern, the field mentor, and the university mentor. This session should take place during the last semester of the internship program and should be sponsored by the university.

This feedback session should provide candid observations of the internship experience. It should be directed toward making the university more responsive to the needs of interns and sponsoring districts. It should provide clearer guidelines for intern behavior. It should also give new direction as to the expectations that are held for the sponsoring school districts.

Finally, this document should be signed and dated by the intern, the school superintendent, the field mentor, and the university mentor.

Summary

This chapter has documented the various steps that interns should engage in when setting the stage for their field experience. The internship is usually the capstone course of a master of arts or doctoral program in school administration. It is the ultimate opportunity for graduate students to test their knowledge in a *real-world environment*. This is the time for future administrators to assess their ability to practice leadership. It is a time for you to evaluate your ability to transfer theory into practice. Setting the stage for this experience requires that you are aware of a number of critical issues that will confront you before you experience day one in an administrative office.

To begin with, you must have a clear understanding with your university representatives about the requirements you must meet in order to qualify for your degree. These requirements should be given top priority in the development of your internship experience. If you do not complete these requirements, you will jeopardize the receipt of your degree.

Second, you must gain support for your internship goals from both the university and your sponsoring school district. It is critical that stakeholder groups in both institutions reach a consensus regarding the outcome of your work. Failure to achieve this relationship will have a deleterious effect on your success as an administrative intern. Accomplishing this will not always be easy. The university will insist that your responsibilities be leadership oriented, with a moderate amount of management activities. The sponsoring school district will opt for you to engage in more management activities and minimize your opportunity to take on leadership responsibilities. Of course, there will be compliance and contractual regulations that will bar you from actually doing some of the planned work. In the final analysis, it is imperative that you develop a good working relationship with all of the stakeholder groups and institutions that you must answer to during your internship.

Third, you must design a formal proposal for each of the projects that you will be responsible for implementing. These proposals should be comprehensive documents that give appropriate audiences specific reasons for why the work should be done; how it will benefit student achievement or organizational efficiency; and how human, material, instructional, facility, and financial resources will be used and in what order and quantity. Proposals should also clearly indicate the significance of the work, the methodological design of the project, and how the outcome data will be reported to various appropriate audiences.

These proposals should be formal documents that can be read and understood by a variety of individuals. They should be free of confusing jargon. They should provide all readers with an opportunity to understand what you intend to do as an administrative intern.

Last, you should have a simple, all-inclusive working agreement with the university and sponsoring school district that clearly depicts the roles and responsibilities of all personnel to be involved in the internship experience. This document may not have legal significance, but it can be used as a reminder of what has to be accomplished if your internship is to be successful.

If you properly set the stage for your internship, you should have a successful leadership experience. The next chapter will discuss the leadership role in the internship experience.

CHAPTER 4

Leading, Not
Simply Surviving

A very understandable feeling for anyone first going into any new career is wanting not to fail in the new job. This is certainly the case for you as you work toward the goal of a position as a school principal or assistant principal. After all, you have invested a great deal of time, money, and personal effort to move from a teaching position into a managerial role.

In this chapter, our focus is on helping you to avoid the natural and understandable temptation of looking exclusively at acquiring only the ability to "get by" or survive as a beginning principal. Obviously, with the dedication of substantial resources to becoming a school administrator, you do not wish to fail; you want to keep the position that you worked so hard to achieve. But it is critical that you not look at *survivorship* as your only goal during the early days of your career. After all, you will be hired because people believe you can provide *leadership* for a school.

Too often, those who engage in intern programs have a tendency to look at this time solely as a period in which they can learn a few "tricks of the trade" that will help them get through the first months on the job. Our goal here is to challenge you to move beyond the stage of wanting simply to "survive." Instead, we firmly believe that if you settle for attaining only a level of survivorship, you may never be able to reach the level of work where you can have the greatest impact as a school administrator, namely effective leadership. In this chapter, we ask you to consider some options concerning your developmental needs and concerns as a future school administrator so that you can move comfortably from one level to the next. You want to make sure that you can do tasks typically assigned to school administrators, and also the much more fulfilling role of being a leader who can truly make a difference for a school.

A Suggested Developmental Pattern

There is a natural progression that we all follow when we first move into a new position. Most people start at the level where they want to learn all they can each day so they will not have any problems the next time they walk into their offices. You do not want to be embarrassed by not being able to do the job for which you are hired. If you are like most people going through a university-based program in educational administration, you have already completed all or most of the traditional courses in curriculum development, personnel, supervision, finance, law, school-community relations, and, no doubt, many other areas that are either mandated by your state department of education or by your university. In all cases, the purpose of requiring you to complete these learning experiences is to provide you with a foundation of content about things associated with leading a school. School principals should be instructional leaders, so you learn about curriculum. Administrators make decisions likely to have consequences regarding due process rights for students, parents, and teachers, so you are expected to learn about school law. These are but two examples of how university programs are intended to help you learn about your new chosen field.

We do not suggest that what you learn in traditional university courses is not valuable for preparing you for the future. However, learning to be a principal by memorizing a list of law cases in education is about the same thing as trying to learn how to communicate with native speakers of a language by only memorizing individual vocabulary words in French, Spanish, Japanese, and so forth. If all you learn in a French course is that the word for "house" is *la maison,* you will be quite frustrated if your long-term goal is to become a real estate agent in France or Quebec.

Knowing the conditions to be fulfilled legally in terms of court cases that define church and state relationships is but a small part of what you might have to know and do as a principal when representatives of a group of students approach you to find out if they can hold Bible study sessions during the lunch hour in your school. But, by learning the "rules of grammar" (educational laws, for example) and the basic "vocabulary," you are able to develop a reasonable foundation for further work.

Considering the kinds of technical skills you want to learn during your internship will assist you with this first stage in your development as a leader. Imagine, for example, that you are about to step into a position as a principal or assistant principal, and you want to make sure that you "survive" your first assignment. In the spaces below, list specific activities associated with traditional administrative task areas where you currently feel uncomfortable and wish to learn more during your intern experience:

Task Area: Instructional Supervision

Specific activities in this task area that you wish to learn more about:

_____

_____

_____

_____

_____

Task Area: Curriculum Development

Specific activities in this task area that you wish to learn more about:

_____

_____

_____

_____

_____

Task Area: Budgeting and Finance

Specific activities in this task area that you wish to learn more about:

_____

_____

_____

_____

_____

Task Area: Legal Issues

Specific activities in this task area that you wish to learn more about:

_____

_____

_____

_____

_____

Task Area: Staff Personnel

Specific issues in this task area that you wish to learn more about:

_____

_____

_____

_____

_____

Task Area: Student Personnel (including special education)

Specific issues in this task area that you want to learn more about:

_____

_____

_____

_____

_____

Task Area: Building and Plant Management

Specific issues in this task area that you wish to learn more about:

_____

_____

_____

_____

_____

Task Area: Community Relations

Specific issues in this task area that you wish to learn more about:

_____

_____

_____

_____

_____

Task Area: Other Miscellaneous Responsibilities

Specific issues in this task area that you wish to learn more about:

_____

_____

_____

_____

_____

Now that you have identified the specific skills you hope to learn more about during your internship, you need to make some critical decisions. What are the issues and tasks that you want to learn about first? It is critical to prioritize, because, as the old saying goes, "You can't do everything all at once." Next, you have to decide on some procedures you can follow to learn how to do what you have identified as most critical for your success as a school administrator.

In the space below, describe the five most important skills you wish to acquire during this internship. After each skill, indicate one or more ways in which you might acquire competence in the identified area:

Priority 1: Skill:

_____

_____

Strategy to be followed in refining this skill:

_____

_____

_____

_____

_____

_____

_____

Priority 2: Skill:

_____

_____

Strategy to be followed in refining this skill:

_____

_____

_____

_____

_____

_____

_____

Priority 3: Skill:

_____

_____

Strategy to be followed in refining this skill:

_____

_____

_____

_____

_____

_____

_____

Priority 4: Skill:

_____

_____

Strategy to be followed in refining this skill:

_____

_____

_____

_____

_____

_____

Priority 5: Skill:

_____

_____

Strategy to be followed in refining this skill:

_____

_____

_____

_____

_____

_____

Moving Beyond Management Into Leadership

The preceding activities asked you focus primarily on the kinds of skills and strategies that you believe are necessary for your survival as a beginning school administrator. They are management tasks faced by an assistant principal or principal. No doubt, in your mind and in the minds of many others, your not being able to do these tasks would result in a less than effective school. In fact, not doing some of the things you have identified may even result in your losing a job. They are important. However, just because you are able to "tame" these tasks does not mean that you are an educational leader, and being an educational leader must be the ultimate goal of anyone going into this business. The question now is, "How can I move beyond a focus on management and begin to look at developing my leadership capacity?"

The next step is a most demanding exercise. You have listed all the issues in the field of school administration that you believe will serve as challenges. These are all identified in terms of specific task areas. In this section, you will need to think about your personal values and vision regarding leadership of a school. Begin by answering this general question: "Think of a school that is so good that you would gladly send your own child to it. What are some of the characteristics of that 'good school'?"

_____

_____

_____

_____

_____

_____

_____

A follow-up question might be, "What are some specific behaviors and practices that I would expect to see in an ideal, or good school?"

_____

_____

_____

_____

_____

_____

_____

After you have thought about the general features of your good school, consider some behaviors and practices that you would expect to see in that school. Now, think about and list some of the specific behaviors and practices that you, as an assistant principal or principal, would have to do.

_____

_____

_____

_____

_____

_____

_____

In this next section, consider how these needed leadership behaviors relate to the skills you earlier identified as your highest priorities. In other words, are the skills that you thought were critical to your initial success as an administrator really as important as you first thought? Can you be a leader and not master some managerial skills and tasks?

Take a moment to check over your earlier assumptions. Then note here any skills that may not be quite as essential.

_____

_____

_____

_____

_____

_____

_____

Now, indicate any administrative skills that you believe are more crucial to help you lead a school toward your vision of effectiveness.

_____

_____

_____

_____

_____

_____

_____

Refining Your Leadership Goal

If we make the assumption that you wish not only to survive your initial steps into administration, but also to build a future as a leader, what activities can assist you? Perhaps the first and most critical step in this process will be for you to find someone with whom you can share your goal. This person may be another intern, your university internship supervisor, or the practicing school administrator who works with you during the internship. Or, it may be someone who is not a direct participant in the internship with you. The critical thing is to identify someone with whom you can share the information that we asked you to consider earlier in this chapter. What do you think you need to know and be able to do simply to survive? What are some of your more creative goals for leading an effective school? What skills are not really needed to achieve that vision? And, what skills are needed?

It is not likely that you will ever achieve your long-term goal of leadership if you try to go at this task alone. Whether it is one person serving as a critical friend or mentor, or several colleagues with whom you feel free to have open dialogue, you should identify people who can be around to keep pushing you to achieve goals as a leader. You need "cheerleaders" to push you in your efforts. And you need people who will not hesitate to be critical if you stray from the goals you have established.

In this last section, you may wish to identify certain individuals you believe can be part of your ongoing support group to help you move toward leadership, and not simply stay "stuck" as a survivor.

Summary

In this chapter, we addressed yet another important part of learning through the use of an effective administrative internship. Specifically, we have taken the stance that, while the internship should help you learn certain practical, useful skills that you will need in order not to fail immediately, you should also have loftier goals. In short, our view is that it is too comfortable to learn simply what will keep you from getting fired. Rather, you should never give up the goal of making your school the most effective it can be. You want to be a leader, not simply a survivor.

To that end, we suggested a process for reviewing your goals in two ways. First, we presented a series of steps to follow to identify what you believe are essential managerial skills and tasks that you will need to know as an assistant principal or principal. Next, we urged you to consider a long-term vision of an effective school that you would like to lead. We then asked that you consider what overlaps exist between your views of critical tasks and skills and your ability to implement the larger vision. Finally, we concluded the chapter by noting that, as you continue in your pursuit of excellence, it will be extremely important to share your dreams and goals with others who can help you.

CHAPTER 5

Carrying Out the Internship

Competencies and Skills

Actual participation in the administrative internship can be the most exciting learning encounter of your entire course of study. It is a time for you to spread your leadership wings and see how far you can fly. It is a time for experimentation and assessment. It is a time for honing your leadership skills and enhancing your leadership capabilities. The internship is the ultimate learning experience, the one where you can make your final decision about wanting to become a school administrator.

The Final Outcome

What do you want to be when you complete your internship experience? The answer to this question should be, *an effective school administrator*. This is easier said than done. You must keep in mind that school administration is a complex, multifaceted undertaking that requires a vast array of skills and a high level of competency to meet strict standards. Effective school administrators are moral and social role models and advocates for the youth of our society. They are also professional role models for their staff members. These roles require an individual to be a well-educated and articulate leader.

Effective school administrators are *change agents* who make a difference in their institutions by transforming them into organizations that can respond to the ever-changing social, economic, and political forces that impact their operations. They are also people of *courage,* because they know how and when to take risks for the betterment of their organization and the people they serve. They are *sensitive* to the needs of their staff and work toward empowering their followers to make things happen in the organization. Effective school administrators are *driven by a set of core values* that influence the way they behave. They are also *lifelong learners* who learn from their mistakes as well as their successes. And they have the *ability to frame and deal with the complex problems* that challenge the achievement of their organizational goals. Finally, effective school administrators are *visionaries*. They have the ability to convert their dreams for the future into viable activities that their followers are willing to believe in and work for.

Thus if your goal is to become an effective school administrator, it would be in your best interest to craft an internship experience that challenges all of the standards, competencies, and skills related to the characteristics mentioned above. You will need to participate in specific experiences that can help you determine how well you measure up to the skill expectations held for an effective school administrator.

Leadership Skills for the 21st Century

What standards and skills are necessary for you to be a successful school administrator in the 21st century? There could be 50 different answers, since the states' certification and licensure requirements are individually crafted for their own needs. However, a number of national associations and professional groups have developed lists of standards and skills that reflect the general expectations that will be held of effective school administrators in the future. It is significant to note that while state requirements are extremely important in directing and dictating what you should know to receive your certification, these national associations and groups are equally important in helping you to focus your attention on what you must be able to do in order to fulfill your promise of effective leadership.

The Interstate School Leaders Licensure Consortium (ISLLC), under the auspices of the Council of Chief State School Officers, has conducted one such effort. The ISLLC standards represent a major effort to bring together a common core of knowledge regarding school administration leadership standards. ISLLC shows how these standards relate to the operation of an effective school. The ISLLC standards appear in Figure 5.1. The National Association of Secondary School Principals (NASSP) has also designed a series of skill dimensions for "Selecting and Developing the 21st Century Principal" (see Figure 5.2). These skills are an excellent complement to the ISLLC standards and provide an additional level of specificity for defining appropriate leadership behavior in our nation's schools.

If your internship experience is to benefit your endeavor to be an effective school administrator, you should consider using such standards and skill arrays as a way to determine the types of activities in which you should participate. You should also use them in assessing the value of the activities in which you are assigned to participate.

Figure 5.1. Interstate School Leaders Licensure Consortium

Standards for School Leaders

Standard 1

A school administrator is an educational leader who promotes the success of all students by *facilitating the development, articulation, implementation, and stewardship of a vision of learning that is shared and supported by the school community.*

Standard 2

A school administrator is an educational leader who promotes the success of all students by *advocating, nurturing, and sustaining a school culture and instructional program conducive to student learning and staff professional growth.*

Standard 3

A school administrator is an educational leader who promotes the success of all students by *ensuring management of the organization, operations, and resources for a safe, efficient, and effective learning environment.*

Standard 4

A school administrator is an educational leader who promotes the success of all students by *collaborating with families and community members, responding to diverse community interests and needs, and mobilizing community resources.*

Standard 5

A school administrator is an educational leader who promotes the success of all students by *acting with integrity, fairness, and in an ethical manner.*

Standard 6

A school administrator is an educational leader who promotes the success of all students by *understanding, responding to, and influencing the larger political, social, economic, legal, and cultural context.*

SOURCE: Interstate School Leaders Licensure Consortium. (1996). *Standards for school leaders.* Washington, DC: Council of Chief State School Officers.

Figure 5.2. National Association of Secondary School Principals

---

Skill Dimensions for Selecting and Developing the 21st-Century Principal

Educational Leadership

- Setting Instructional Direction
- Teamwork
- Sensitivity

Resolving Complex Problems

- Judgment
- Results Orientation
- Organizational Ability

Communication

- Oral Communication
- Written Communication

Developing Self and Others

- Development of Others
- Understanding Own Strengths and Weaknesses

SOURCE: National Association of Secondary School Principals. (1999, August). *Selecting and developing the 21st century principal: Program skills.* Washington, DC: Author.

From the Field 5.1

Interns are often assigned specific types of activities that sponsoring building administrators believe are important experiences for developing practical knowledge (e.g., scheduling the building, following up on student absenteeism, overseeing evening activities, etc.). Also, some interns are given an opportunity to participate in certain activities that they feel are of special interest to their personal development as school administrators (e.g., researching and writing a new discipline policy, working with a group of parents on the development of a volunteer program, inservicing a group of supervisors on a new classroom observation technique, etc.). It is important to determine if the activity is making an enriching contribution to your skill development, whether it is assigned or voluntary. If you have specific standards or skill arrays in mind, this will greatly enhance your ability to assess the importance of each activity.

Guiding the Implementation
of an Internship

As you begin to plan your internship experience, there are several overarching principles that you should use to form the basic platform of your experience. These principles will act as a structure that you can rely on for continuous guidance throughout your internship. In essence, they represent general principles for all school administrators' performance regardless of their position or status.

1. Remember that your leadership behavior and decision making must always focus on the needs of students.

2. Remember that you are responsible for leading your staff by providing them with every opportunity to be involved in the decision-making activities that ultimately affect student outcomes. Teamwork is essential to institutional success.

3. Be a visionary leader. Always make sure your staff knows and understands your meaning of the future.

4. Be aware of the forces of change and their impact on the complexity of your position, as well as the needs of your institution.

5. Strive to motivate yourself and your staff to exceed existing limits.

6. Be reflective. Always assess the impact of your behavior and decision making on others. Always reflect on how others behave toward you and the impact of your decision making.

Exercise

How would you apply each of the aforementioned principles to your internship situation?

Student needs:

_____

_____

_____

Leading the staff:

_____

_____

_____

Being a visionary leader:

_____

_____

_____

Dealing with the forces of change:

_____

_____

_____

Motivating self and others:

_____

_____

_____

Being reflective:

_____

_____

_____

Defining Standards for Internship Practice

Armed with a strong set of guiding principles, your next step should be to identify a set of standards that you can employ to measure your growth as a school leader. While they standards might be individualistic in nature, the ISLLC standards are certainly general enough for everyone to use as a starting point. You might want to alter them in areas where they do not meet your unique needs at the internship site. But for starters let's use them to illustrate how standards might work in a practical way at your internship site.

Standard 1

A school administrator is an educational leader who promotes the success of all students by *facilitating the development, articulation, implementation, and stewardship of a vision of learning that is shared and supported by the school community.* (Interstate School Leaders Licensure Consortium [ISLLC], 1996)

This standard expects a school administrator to believe that all students can learn and will respond positively to high expectations. It also suggests that effective school administrators will work continually to improve the way their schools improve, to provide students with thorough and efficient learning opportunities. This standard asks administrators continually to examine and reflect upon their beliefs and practices when it comes to their school's obligations to the community.

What are the major characteristics of your vision for student learning?

_____

_____

_____

One of the first things you must do is determine the sum and substance of the school district and school building administrations' visions for student learning. You must have a clear and articulate understanding of where your vision for student learning stands in relation to both of both these existing structures. You must identify points of agreement and disagreement. It is OK to have points of disagreement (that's what helps make the world go 'round), but you must be ready to defend your different ideas. Your clarity about this relationship will help guide your approach to making decisions and explaining your actions.

From the Field 5.2

Sometimes district and/or building-level administrators do not have a definable or recognizable vision for student learning. On the other hand, although they may have such visions they may not exhibit them in their ongoing behavior because too many extrinsic forces cause them to behave in other ways. First, understand that this phenomenon is not uncommon. Second, and more important, do not let such situations affect your behavior. It is extremely important for you to test your vision for student learning during the internship experience. You must be able to experience whether staff members are willing to take up the cause that you profess is the "right way" to educate our youth. You must have positive experiences that will help you defend or change your way of thinking.

Standard 2

A school administrator is an educational leader who promotes the success of all students by *advocating, nurturing, and sustaining a school culture and instructional program conducive to student learning and staff professional growth.* (ISLLC, 1996)

This standard expects school administrators to understand that the basic reason for schooling is student learning. It challenges administrators to think of a variety of ways that students can learn. It advocates that school administrators should think of their students, staff, and themselves as lifelong learners. It asks school administrators to seek ways of providing staff with professional development opportunities that will create beneficial diversity within the entire school community.

How would you define a school culture that is conducive to student learning?

_____

_____

_____

How would you define an instructional program that is conducive to student learning?

_____

_____

_____

Well in advance of beginning your internship experience, you should have a good understanding of the impact of school culture on student learning at your internship site. With permission, you should visit the site when school is in session. You should walk around the school's hallways and talk with students and teachers. See if you can gain insight to their opinions about the type of culture they subsist in, whether there are any barriers to student learning, how accomplishments (student and staff) are celebrated, how curriculum decisions are made, how diversity is handled, the extent to which technology is relied on for instruction and classroom management, how fairly people are treated, and how individuals are respected for their work. Information regarding the school culture and climate should have a profound impact on how you go about your work as an administrative intern.

From the Field 5.3

Remember that school cultures and instructional programs are developed over a very long time period. They are part of the tradition of the district and the school building. In many instances, you will be working with individuals who played an important role in developing such cultures and programs. You have to be very cautious about how you react to the culture and program you find. Remember, if you criticize any element of the culture or program, you may be doing so to the individual who was responsible for its creation. Be very careful about what you say and to whom you say it. It is safe to assume that in your capacity as an administrative intern you will not have enough influence to change the school culture or its instructional program, unless you are involved in a project that the stakeholders of the institution had planned to conduct well before your arrival. At this juncture it is OK to compliment them on their ability to project into the future.

Standard 3

A school administrator is an educational leader who promotes the success of all students by *ensuring management of the organization, operations, and resources for a safe, efficient, and effective learning environment.* (ISLLC, 1996)

This standard expects school administrators to make management decisions that will influence quality instruction and student learning. It challenges administrators to create partnerships with staff and other stakeholders in the design and delivery of instructional services to students.

How would you characterize a safe, efficient, and effective learning environment?

_____

_____

_____

During your internship experience it is very important that you learn how to make and assess informed management decisions. You must be able to ascertain what procedures are necessary to maximize student learning opportunities. You must become aware of the nature and types of resources that administrators have at their disposal to manage and create an effective and efficient organization. You must also be aware of alternative ways to use resources so that you can facilitate the achievement of your organizational goals in efficient and effective ways.

From the Field 5.4

Whether you are interning in a wealthy district or one of want, the human, financial, and material resources should be considered scarce and precious. They are to be used only after careful planning and articulate decision making. Being a creative resource manager will always have a positive effect on your anticipated goals. The creative use of resources does not mean making "cheap" or "bottom-line" decisions. It means being prudent when you can achieve the same outcome by exerting less pressure on your finite resources.

Standard 4

A school administrator is an educational leader who promotes the success of all students by *collaborating with families and community members, responding to diverse community interests and needs, and mobilizing community resources.* (ISLLC, 1996)

This standard requires school administrators to appreciate the place of the school district in the community as a whole. Administrators must understand that communicating and working with students' families is an extremely important part of the formal education process. They must also understand that an informed community is as important a resource for achieving school goals as an appropriate instructional program is.

How would you collaborate with families and community members to better educate the students at your intern site?

_____

_____

_____

What elements make up diverse community interests and needs?

_____

_____

_____

How would you define such diverse interest and needs for the community that is served by your internship site?

_____

_____

_____

How would you mobilize community resources in your internship site for the betterment of students' educational opportunities?

_____

_____

_____

The formal education received through schooling is only one of the types of education that students need in order to succeed in life. Their informal education is no less important, and may have a bigger impact on their learning than their schooling does. There should be a concerted effort by school administrators to bridge the gap between the formal and informal learning systems. During your internship experience you should explore and experiment with collaborating with parents and community. Over the past four decades there has been a tremendous deterioration in the school-community relationship. Educators' relationships with parents have also gone downhill. Acquiring experience and information on how to restart this once powerful relationship for the benefit of students, the community, and the education system will enhance your future success as an administrator.

From the Field 5.5

Understanding how your internship site mobilizes and uses community resources is extremely important. In many districts, such relationships are crucial to how a community accepts change in procedures, views student outcomes, and lends support for impending reforms. But you must remember that good public relations begins with HOW YOU TREAT PEOPLE, NOT HOW MUCH INFORMATION YOU FEED THEM. Too often we send home a newsletter, but make it difficult for parents and other caregivers to talk to us. Look very carefully at how the teachers and administration treat parents and community members in face-to-face encounters.

Standard 5

A school administrator is an educational leader who promotes the success of all students by *acting with integrity, fairness, and in an ethical manner.* (ISLLC, 1996)

This standard expects school administrators to be democratic in the conduct of their duties. They should be honest and fair in the enactment of their roles. They must treat all staff equally. They must apply the rules and regulations of their school equitably and fairly. Their decision making must be free of any intrinsic or extrinsic forces that may cause them to treat people unfairly.

Can you think of any examples of how administrators do not conduct their office in an honest, fair, and ethical manner?

_____

_____

_____

What kinds of forces might cause administrators to behave unfairly or unethically?

_____

_____

_____

During the course of your internship experience you must project your own personal and professional code of ethics. Remember, you are an intern and you are going to make mistakes. Admit to those mistakes and then correct them. Be honest and fair with students and staff. Try not to be embarrassed by your actions. Learn how to take constructive criticism. Be reflective about your actions. Make sure you assess how your decisions have impacted others. Try to understand why students and/or staff are reacting toward you in a certain manner. Remember, honesty is the best policy, regardless of the consequences.

Be very observant of your mentor's ethical manner, as well as that of other administrators practicing at your internship site. It is not your place to respond to what you observe, however; distance yourself from any nefarious practices that you see.

From the Field 5.6

Sometimes administrators will take the "low road" and do things to please a certain faction of staff, parents, or community residents. In doing so, they compromise their ethics. This may accord them a place in the sun for a short time, but in the long run, experience tells us that actions like this can backfire and result in serious consequences.

What people think of you starts with your integrity, fairness, and ethical manner. If you lose the trust of your staff, parents, and/or the community, it is almost impossible to restore it fully. Effective leaders do the right thing. Sometime people do not agree with the right thing, but that's their problem, not yours. As the saying goes, you never get a second change to make a first impression.

Your job is to educate the students of your school building better, not to run a popularity contest. Do not sacrifice your code of ethics for a brief moment of popularity.

Standard 6

A school administrator is an educational leader who promotes the success of all students by *understanding, responding to, and influenc-*

ing the larger political, social, economic, legal, and cultural context.
(ISLLC, 1996)

Effective school administrators must understand that their school districts and buildings are not islands detached from the mainland. They must understand that these institutions are an integral part of a complex political, economic, and social system. As such, they are susceptible to the decision-making powers of other institutions. Because they are partly funded by government, their operation must comply with rules and regulations enacted by society's lawmakers. All of this means that school administrators must maintain a continuing dialogue with members of those institutions that ultimately impact education. They must also be responsive in the use of the legal system as a protector of their students and staffs.

In addition, school administrators should realize that if they reach out, there are many educational institutions that are in close enough proximity to establish a networking relationship to discuss solutions to current issues and procedures. Such network relationships are helpful in identifying alternative solutions to common problems. You do not have to work in isolation or "reinvent the wheel." Networks also provide an opportunity to develop lobbying partnerships to convince government or other institutions to make decisions in favor of quality education.

How would you characterize the relationship your internship site has with local, state and federal institutions?

Local: _____

_____

_____

State: _____

_____

_____

Federal: _____

_____

_____

What types of common activities could you engage in with administrators of neighboring school districts?

_____

_____

_____

It is probable that internship activities related to this standard might be limited, if not completely silent. Relationships with outside institutions are most likely to take place at the district level. These relationships are often delicate and very involved; consequently, it would not be common for interns to be actively involved in them. However, similar relationships that occur at the building level (curriculum consortia, roundtable meetings, etc.) might provide more acceptable networking activities for you. You should inquire about such out-of-building activities and try to experience them even if it is in an observation capacity. This might involve your attendance at a monthly meeting of regional principals or your taking part in a multischool discussion about violence protection systems.

Skill Development Through the Internship Experience

The next step in carrying out your internship experience is to identify the specific skills that you should be developing and enhancing as you participate in projects and assigned activities. By doing this you will be able to monitor the progress of your skill development throughout your experience.

As in the section on standards, it is assumed that the actual skills you identify will be those that relate specifically to your individual internship situation. Consequently, we will use the skills from NASSP's 21st Century School Administrator Skills Program to illustrate how these skills might look in practice at your internship site.

Educational Leadership Skills

Setting Instructional Direction. Skills in this area relate to improving the teaching and learning process. Projects related to these skills include designing and implementing new instructional programs or improving existing programs to enhance student learning. The area also includes crafting a vision with corresponding goals and motivating staff to accept them as guiding forces for their contributions and participation. These are some of the most important skills that effective school administrators can possess. They are important for setting an organizational direction. They are directed at the very core of what schooling is about and how leaders develop a following to achieve a set of common goals.

What are some of the projects/activities related to your internship that will enhance your instructional direction skills?

_____

_____

_____

Teamwork. Teamwork skills are related to such activities as facilitating group processes in shared decision making; encouraging staff to be involved in team efforts; using group activities as a way to recognize team accomplishments; using group activities to build self-esteem; and planning and conducting effective meetings. The nature of education is becoming more complex each academic year. The individual teacher can no longer conduct class lessons in isolation. Lifelong learning needs have made it necessary for professional staff members to work closely together in developing and implementing viable learning opportunities. Effective leaders must possess the ability to motive and lead their staff in productive teamwork.

What are some of the projects/activities related to your internship that will enhance your teamwork skills?

_____

_____

_____

Sensitivity. Being sensitive means that you can anticipate and understand the needs and concerns of your staff; can tactfully handle conflict resolution; can relate to a staff member's job-related emotional stress; know how to communicate information with discretion; and know how to relate to the ethnic, cultural, and religious diversity that exists on your staff, among your students, and in the community your building serves. These skills are major image builders for the school administrator. They also relate to some of the most delicate situations with which leaders can find themselves confronted.

What are some of the projects/activities related to your internship that will enhance your sensitivity skills?

_____

_____

_____

Resolving Complex Problems

Judgment. Judgment skills relate to your ability to use the upper levels of the cognitive domain. They speak about your effectiveness in drawing logical conclusions; effecting good decisions based on existing information; gathering, analyzing, and interpreting complex data; and prioritizing critical issues. Such high-order skills are essential for the day-to-day operation of a building, as well as the long-term activities that ensure a continual, positive move in the direction of achieving your vision.

What are some of the projects/activities related to your internship that will enhance your judgment skills?

_____

_____

_____

Results Orientation. These skills relate to your ability to assume leadership responsibility; make decisions within an appropriate time frame; and balance short- and long-term issues. Do not accept a position of leadership responsibility unless you really want to be a leader. If you cannot make a decision, do not become a leader. The daily routine of a leader is fraught with decision making that often impacts the lives of many individuals. You must be ready, willing, and able to decide and defend what should be happening, while being consistent with your actions.

What are some of the projects/activities related to your internship that will enhance your results orientation skills?

_____

_____

_____

Organizational Ability. These skills relate to your ability to use human, material, and financial resources judiciously; monitor projects; delegate work; utilize the practical applications of organizational theory; use strategic planning skills; interpret local, state, and federal policies and regulations for practical application in the building; apply education law to practice; develop and use a budgeting process; and apply the basic principles of financial management and cost accounting. Remember that every leader is also a manager to some extent. You must master skills such as these to be an effective manager.

What are some of the projects/activities related to your internship that will enhance your organizational ability skills?

_____

_____

_____

Communication Skills

Oral Communication. These skills are related to your ability to make clear and easy-to-understand oral presentations; engage students, staff, and the community in ways that motivate them to reflect upon and support the building's mission; engage individuals and groups in a positive manner; and listen actively and respond appropriately to the ideas and opinions of others. Remember you are the spokesperson for your staff and students when it comes to education in your building. Consequently, you must be an effective public speaker, able to think well and fast on your feet.

What are some of the projects/activities related to your internship that will enhance your oral communication skills?

_____

_____

_____

Written Communication. If you must be an effective speaker, you must also be an effective writer. These skills relate to your ability to express ideas clearly in writing; demonstrate proficiency with the written word; write for diverse audiences; and design and implement an effective public relations program in conjunction with your oral communication skills.

What are some of the projects/activities related to your internship that will enhance your written communication skills?

_____

_____

_____

Developing Self and Others

Development of Others. These skills are related to your ability to be a mentor, coach, and teacher for your staff members: conduct appropriate and meaningful classroom observations, providing meaningful feedback to your staff regarding their teaching ability, and knowing the professional inservice needs of your staff and how to address those needs.

What are some of the projects/activities related to your internship that will enhance your mentoring and coaching skills?

_____

_____

_____

Understanding Your Own Strengths and Weaknesses. These skills relate to your ability to reflect on your own practice and determine the impact you are having on students, staff, administration, parents, and the community. They also relate to your ability to reflect on your own professional needs and how they should be addressed. They could also be referred to as your lifelong-learner skills. You are a role model. What you want your staff and students to do, you should be able to do as well. You will be unofficially observed during every possible moment of your practice. If you are a reflective administrator, you will know what others think about you. Then you will be prepared to be proactive about improving yourself.

What are some of the projects/activities related to your internship that will enhance your reflective practice and lifelong-learner skills?

_____

_____

_____

Summary

This chapter was designed to help you think about three major ingredients for a productive internship. First, we identified some guiding principles that will help you set a foundation for the organization and implementation of your internship experience. Second, we used the ISLLC standards to illustrate how standards can help you define the specific outcome goals you should have prior to starting your internship experience. Finally, we used the NASSP skills for 21st-century principals to illustrate the types of skills you should seek to develop during your internship experience. Throughout the chapter you have been reminded that the specific guiding principles, standards, and skills can be different for your unique experience. What was presented here was an illustration of how to think about these elements when you are crafting your own. Whatever you use to determine your specific set of principles, standards, and skills, keep in mind that in our opinion this is a necessary undertaking if you are to be successful.

CHAPTER**6**

The Role of the
University Supervisor

From the Field 6.1

Dr. Carlos Ochoa recently retired after 19 years as the superintendent of the Capital City Local Schools. Before that, he had several years as a very successful principal, assistant principal, and teacher, not only in Capital City Local, but also in three other school districts in the state. He was highly regarded by so many people that it was not surprising that he recently started a new career as a faculty member at Capital State University in their department of educational administration and supervision. After all, Carlos had significant experiences to share, and it was generally understood that CSU had a faculty made up largely of bright young researchers who had spent practically no time out "in the trenches" as public school administrators, or even as teachers.

Dr. Ochoa's primary responsibility as a new faculty member was to teach three courses. One was a general introduction to administration, one was a seminar on current issues, and the third was to be the internship required of all students seeking state certification as administrators. He found the planning for the two regular courses to be easier than he expected. He was well read, and his predecessor on the CSU faculty had given him a lot of great material to use in his courses. The toughest part of his assignment was directing the internship, an activity that he had at first believed to be a very easy job given the fact that all he had to do was to "go out to schools now and then and see the interns if he had time." At least that was what the university department chair had told him. After a week on the job, Carlos realized that if he really wanted to help students grow into administrative roles, he would have to do much more. The question now was, "What?"

As we have noted throughout the earlier chapters of this book, the internship is a critical part of the administrator preparation programs at most universities. It is, therefore, a required "class" in most states for those who wish to achieve licensure or certification as a school administrator. Academic credit is granted, grades are assigned, and expectations are established to ensure that the internship conforms to the standards of the university, graduate school, and academic department of the institution that houses the administrator preparation program. On the other hand, the administrative internship is not like a traditional university course. It does not feel or look like learning experiences that meet regularly in university lecture halls or seminar rooms, where professors control content and class activities, and where student learning is assessed through periodic written examinations and scholarly papers. In short, the internship required of aspiring school administrators in many universities suffers a kind of "identity crisis" in that it is not always clear if it is a respected part of the university curriculum or simply an "add-on" tolerated because "the state requires it for certification."

As a result of this ambiguity, the role of the university faculty member assigned the responsibility of coordinating, leading, or supervising the administrative internship is a very difficult one. In this chapter, our goal is to bring about greater understanding of what should be considered as part of the responsibilities and role of the university supervisor. Our hope is that this discussion will help universities improve their practices; but even more important, we want to be able to provide you, as an intern, with further appreciation of how a critical participant in your field-based learning activity might be an even more effective and valuable resource.

In this chapter, we begin by looking at what it means to coordinate the overall internship for a university. Second, we offer some suggestions for what might be included when developing periodic seminars that are meant to accompany the field experiences of the internship. Next, we talk about special skills and behaviors that need to be demonstrated by the university supervisor who serves as a mentor to interns. Finally, we conclude by identifying a set of specific role expectations for the university or coordinator.

Periodic Seminars for Interns

The essence of an internship for aspiring school administrators is the time spent out in the field engaged in tasks normally required of principals and assistant principals in schools. As a result, many who enroll in internships are surprised to find out that, in most instances, the university supervisor of the internship will typically also require those who are currently enrolled in the field experience to attend periodic meetings of an intern seminar, often held on the university campus. In some cases, the seminar location floats from site to site in the public schools in which interns currently work. Depending on the circumstances at an individual institution, the meetings of the seminar might be scheduled once each month during a term or perhaps only two or three times during the entire semester or quarter. Decisions on frequency of meetings might be dictated by such local factors as the number of interns enrolled in a given term or by the size of the geographic area in which the interns are dispersed. In a setting where students are working in schools across a large portion of a state, it may be feasible to bring the group together on only a few occasions; when interns all work in the same district, more frequent seminars might be convened.

Regardless of the exact circumstances in any specific location, the seminar is an important part of the intern experience. The university supervisor or coordinator plays a major role in ensuring that this activity is a positive part of the overall program of field-based learning. Basically, the internship seminar has the following potential objectives:

1. Reaffirm initial goals and objectives

2. Formative evaluation

3. Network building

4. Collegial learning

Reaffirm Initial Goals and Objectives

The assumption is that, before the internship has begun, each person enrolled in the experience will have already determined set of personal goals and objectives to be achieved while working in the field. In addition, the university offering the internship has a set of learning objectives stated as expectations for student performance during the internship. The intern seminar, whether held weekly, monthly, or less frequently, can be a time when interns reflect on their progress toward meeting those goals, objectives, and expectations.

As an example, an individual intern may place a high priority on addressing one of the potential goals we noted earlier, in Chapter 2, namely that the internship may be used as a time to test personal commitment to the field of administration. If this were an intern's objective, the seminar sessions could easily be viewed as benchmarking times when the intern might take stock of where he or she might be relative to "testing personal commitment."

In the space below, identify one or more personal objectives that you have identified as part of your intern experience. As the year progresses, and as you engage in periodic meetings of the intern seminar, you may wish to make some notes for yourself regarding how well you are proceeding toward these personal goals.

In addition, the seminar sessions can be moments when you can assess your progress toward achieving one or more of the internship objectives established by the university. For example, the course objectives might state that, by the end of the internship, you would be able to demonstrate skill in conducting special education conferences required by law. In the space below, note any objectives that have been specified by others for the internship and, as the internship continues, indicate how well you are addressing these expectations.

Formative Evaluation

While the setting of goals and objectives to guide the internship at the beginning of the experience is good practice, learning in the field is a dynamic activity. As a result, new professional issues often arise, and priorities often change after the practicum has begun. For example, consider the way in which the tragic events of recent shootings on school campuses across the nation suddenly placed school violence and safety issues on a higher plane than they had ever been in American education. Obviously, if you had been engaged in an internship during the spring of 1999, after the Columbine High School tragedy, you would have suddenly been involved with more crisis management planning than you may have imagined when the university term began in midwinter.

Periodic seminars during the course of the internship can be used as opportunities for you and your colleagues to check on how well you are doing with your established goals, as noted in the previous section. In addition, these meetings can also be times to engage in formative evaluation of the learning experience, or midcourse corrections. While dramatic events such as school violence may (fortunately) be rare occurrences, there are other situations that arise in the world of schools that may cause you to adjust your thinking about what you hope to learn from your time in the field. New legislation may be mandated at the state or federal level, tax levies may pass (or not pass) and change funding priorities in the schools, and so forth.

In the space below, keep track of major events that may have an effect on the priorities and objectives that you have established for your internship. Along with these issues, make a note of how other goals or objectives established for you learning experience may change.

Network Building

Many people assume that the internship is an independent learning experience. In fact, the intern must engage in the field-based learning activities as an individual, but that is only part of the potential to be realized through this form of learning. When the university supervisor or coordinator brings together those who are currently enrolled in the internship for periodic seminars, another important dimension is added.

When interns gather once a week, month, or some other established time, they are able to share common experiences related to the things they have observed and learned while playing the role of school administrator. The old saying that "the grass always appears greener in the neighbor's yard" begins to take on a certain reality when interns begin to discuss the kinds of problems they faced but thought were unique to the schools or districts in which they are working.

As your internship progresses, use the space below to note some of the contacts that you make with other interns, your field mentor, other administrators with whom you interact, and so forth. (Make certain to keep phone numbers and e-mail addresses!)

_____

_____

_____

_____

_____

_____

_____

_____

Collegial Learning

In many old adventure movies, there is often a portrayal of leaders as people who can "do it all by themselves," and that relying on others is a sign of weakness. This might be termed the "John Wayne Syndrome," the "Lone Ranger Approach to Leadership," or "Problem Solving as Indiana Jones." Unfortunately, it is an image that is often alive and well in school administrators' offices across the nation. And the corresponding notion—that asking other people for help with complex problems makes a person a "wimp"—is another unfortunate part of the culture of school administration that has been adopted by many. Principals do not want to appear incompetent or unable to deal with their assignments because they ask others to help them from time to time.

The fact is, no good leader ever ran an effective organization without listening to others and consulting with people who might have insights into the ways in which complex problems might be approached. And, if anything can be predicted in absolute terms about the future of schools and school administrators, problems and challenges will increase and become even more complex. The weakest leaders are likely to be the most ineffective, and ineffectiveness in many instances may be linked to a person's inability to communicate with others and develop collegial relationships with peers. The days of the "action hero" being all things to all people all the time are over, if those days ever existed in the past.

Periodic meetings with the others now serving as interns at your university are a way to begin acquiring the necessary skills for forming collegial relationships. As the internship experience progresses and you begin to face greater numbers of problems and challenges for which there are no absolutely "correct answers" or "quick fixes," you can begin to talk with others who are "in the same boat." The intern seminars can therefore become a starting point for the development of true collegial learning and problem solving.

In the space below, take notes regarding issues that you encounter while out in the field but wish to discuss with other interns during your seminar meetings this year.

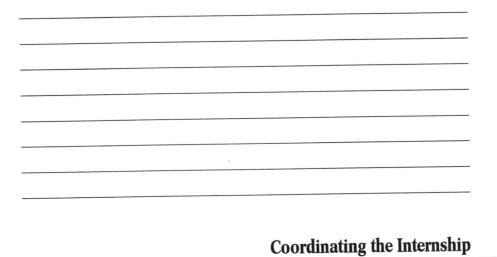

Coordinating the Internship

The central duty of the university faculty member who takes on the role of supervisor of administrative internships is to coordinate all of the activities associated with operating an effective field-based learning experience. Being responsible for supervising such a program is quite different from any other form of university teaching. Traditional instructional roles feature mostly one-way communication techniques where the teacher imparts knowledge to the students. In contrast, coordinating an internship requires that someone help create the conditions in which interns, as students, are able to become the source of their own learning as they work in the field.

In order to ensure that students both achieve personal goals and meet the standards established by the state certification or licensure agency and the university, the supervisor has several responsibilities. First, the supervisor must know precisely what the state's minimum requirements are. Second, the supervisor must be well versed in the specific requirements of the university. Third, the supervisor must be sensitive to the needs of individual aspiring administrators as they engage in the internship.

Knowledge of State Requirements

Until recently, the duty of the university supervisor overseeing state mandates requiring the internship was a relatively simple task. The typical requirement for the planned field experience or internship was stated only in quantifiable terms. For example, candidates for the principalship would need to complete an internship where a minimum of 150 clock hours would be spent in the field studying under the direct supervision of a practicing school administrator. Such policies are relatively easy to enforce, but they are reviewed exclusively from the perspective of counting the hours spent serving as interns; they did little to determine the quality of learning of administrative practice. In recent years, a shift has occurred in many states, prompted in large measure by the efforts of the National Policy Board for Educational Administration and the Interstate Leadership Licensure Consortium. These agencies and several states have emphasized the need for principal preparation to be guided not by mere counting of classes or hours in internships, but rather through the demonstration of whether or not aspiring administrators appear to be learning anything about their chosen future career.

The implication of this change in the nature of state requirements for the internship is that the role of the university supervisor or coordinator has changed significantly. In the past, the supervisor was expected to be a book-keeper who made certain that each intern spent the requisite amount of hours in the field. Now, in addition to this type of accounting duty, in many states the supervisor is also responsible for ensuring that the activities conducted by the intern will contribute to a deeper understanding of administrative practice. In the past, interns could complete their "class" by sorting paper and licking envelopes in the main office. Now, the expectation is that they will acquire skills in making a school into a more effective learning organization for students. That means that the university supervisor has a much different job.

Write a brief description of what your state education agency requires in the internship in which you are enrolled. Is this expressed only in terms of hours in the field? Or is there a stated expectation of certain outcomes to be achieved as a result of the experience? What are the outcomes?

_____

_____

_____

_____

_____

_____

University Requirements

As noted in Chapter 2, in most cases across the country, the administrative internship is actually classified as a regular university graduate-level course in which students must enroll as they would for the course in supervision, law, or finance. The university faculty member assigned to this course, then, is responsible for overseeing all aspects of the instructional experience. More details on this will be presented at the close of this chapter.

The internship supervisor or coordinator should ensure that this important learning experience meets university standards and expectations. In addition, the supervisor must also ensure that the value of the internship as a way for the candidate to achieve the multiple goals and outcomes presented in Chapter 2 is maintained. In short, the supervisor must safeguard the academic and practical values of this course.

The university internship supervisor also must make certain that, as a course, the internship conforms to all normal standards expected by any academic experience offered by the institution. At times this may put the field experience at odds with university demands. For example, a frequent reality is that the time during which it is possible for the intern to complete assigned tasks in the field is not compatible with the university calendar. An intern may be assigned the task of overseeing the final inventory of textbooks in a school and reporting this to appropriate authorities by June 1. Unfortunately, the university spring semester might end on May 15. In short, the intern might still be engaged in work after a grade must be turned in to the campus registrar. It is important that the supervisor exercise appropriate judgment to ensure that the intern is not jeopardized and that the policies of the university are addressed.

If you are serving as a university faculty member assigned the responsibility of supervising or coordinating the administrative internship, write down any additional challenges that you might face with regard to making sure that the internship conforms to university requirements. These might be in such areas as scheduling, grade reporting deadlines, and so forth.

Individual Needs

It is important that state requirements and university standards are respected in the ways in which the administrative internship is carried out. However, the most important "audience" to be satisfied in a well-conceived internship must be the clients of the field experience, namely the interns themselves. Therefore, a central duty of the person responsible for supervising the internship must be to develop sensitivity to each person enrolled in the experience. This may seem like a challenge beyond the limits of the many internship programs where only one faculty member is expected to supervise and work with as many as 30 interns placed in schools across a large geographic area. Nevertheless, if the goal of an internship is to serve as a learning experience for each intern enrolled, attention must be paid to individual needs.

Some institutions have initiated the use of assessment techniques as part of their regular preservice principal preparation programs as a way to identify specific strengths and weaknesses of administrative candidates. Two of these programs that are now available across the nation are the Assessment Center of the National Association of Secondary School Principals, and the Professional Development Inventory developed by the National Association of Elementary School Principals. Each of these processes is designed to enable practicing and aspiring administrators to engage in sessions in which, through the completion of a series of simulated job-related tasks and activities, they are presented with profiles of their greatest skills in certain administrative tasks areas. In addition, individuals who undergo the assessment process are also given an indication of where they need to focus attention in their personal professional development to increase their ability to carry out other administrative tasks.

The assessment techniques noted above are powerful tools that could assist the university supervisor to identify specific skill areas that need further refinement through the activities in an internship. However, assessment in this formal sense is costly; while prices differ, depending upon local circumstances, neither the NASSP nor the NAESP programs are available for much less than $300 per participant.

Less costly approaches to helping interns identify areas of personal need are available. Again, the National Association of Elementary School Principals (NAESP) has a publication available, *Proficiencies for Principals* (NAESP, 1991). This document includes a section where individuals are invited to engage in a self-review of leadership skills that may call for additional development.

Regardless of the tool selected, activities such as the personal assessment and review techniques noted above may be helpful to the internship supervisor in assisting interns to specify skill and knowledge areas that they believe need further attention in their internships. If you are a university supervisor, indicate in the space below the ways in which you believe you may be able to get to know the individual needs of your administrative interns. If you are an intern, indicate the ways in which you may be able to describe your specific concerns and needs to your university supervisor.

Specific Duties of the Supervisor

The description of the role and responsibilities of the university faculty member in charge of the administrative internship has so far focused on broad responsibilities. In this last section of the chapter, we note some of the elements that may be found in the typical job description of anyone who takes on this important role in the preservice preparation program for future school principals.

One of the first duties of the internship coordinator is to meet with students, either individually or in small groups, during the academic term prior to the one in which they intend to enroll in the internship at the university. There are several purposes of these meetings. First, they are a way to ensure that prospective interns appreciate the purposes, procedures, and expectations associated with the field experience. Second, they are a way for the supervisor to begin to know more about the backgrounds and needs of those with whom she or he will be working in the internship experience. Third, it is through these meetings that the supervisor can assist the individual students to identify appropriate placements for their internships. In some instances, it may be acceptable for interns to serve the field experience in their own schools, with their current principal serving as their field mentor. The supervisor should assist the student in determining if this practice, though technically acceptable, is in the best interest of the intern. Are there ways in which the student might have opportunities to work with administrators in other schools or districts? In other cases, university or state education agency policies might prohibit serving as an intern in the school in which the intern is teaching. In these cases, the supervisor needs to work with candidates to identify acceptable settings, and also to work out a plan in which the intern might be able to continue working as a teacher in one school while engaging in field-based learning in other sites.

Once the initial planning meeting is established with the next term's intern "class," the university supervisor has the responsibilities of course planning similar to any other faculty member preparing for a class. A course syllabus must be developed, with a clear statement of the goals and objectives of the program, performance expectations, and the ways in which intern performance will be assessed so that appropriate grades may be assigned. Regardless of whether the internship is a pass/fail experience or one in which traditional grades (A through F) are assigned, it is critical that enrolled students are aware of these demands at the outset. Third, if they are part of the internship program, the supervisor must develop a schedule of seminars and other special events for which attendance will be required of all interns.

Another key set of responsibilities for the supervisor resides in arranging site visits to interns as the term progresses. In an ideal setting, the intern supervisor should be able to make multiple site visits to each intern during a quarter or semester. In many institutions, however, the supervisor has a large number of assigned interns, a large geographic region to cover, or many other circumstances that make it nearly impossible to visit each person more than once. Nevertheless, we believe that two conditions must be observed, regardless of special local conditions. First, it is critical that each intern be visited on-site at least once during each academic term in which he or she is enrolled in the program. Second, the supervisor needs to make a commitment to be on call for additional visits if warranted. These additional visits might be made based on requests form the field mentor administrators, the interns, or the university internship supervisor or coordinator.

When site visits are made, they need to be substantive sessions, not merely courtesy calls to schools so that there appears to be supervision provided by the university. The supervisor needs to be clear in setting the expectation that, when a site visit is made, it is important for the intern to arrange for the mentor administrator to be present as well. The purpose of the meeting should be a review of the intern's progress toward meeting the goals that have been established by the university, the faculty supervisor, the intern, and the administrator serving as a mentor. In many cases, site visits have been little more than social conversations where the mentor administrator or the faculty supervisor has done little more than chat about common interests. Instead, site meetings are a central part of the actual instructional focus of the internship.

A final major responsibility of the university supervisor of internships involves the actual assigning of a grade to the individual interns. Whether this is a pass/fail determination or the designation of a specific letter grade, the university supervisor will be the person ultimately forwarding a grade report to the registrar of the university. Many debates have been held about the responsibilities of the practitioner mentor administrators who work with the interns on a regular basis: Should they not be the people ultimately responsible for assigning grades? In our judgment, there is no question that the university supervisor should consult with the field administrators to seek advice concerning the success that an intern had during the previous term. However, since the internship is typically classified as a university credit-bearing activity, it is ultimately the responsibility of a faculty member to make a final determination of each student's performance in the "class." The faculty member is fully responsible for such decisions.

In addition to the general duties to be assumed by the university supervisor or coordinator, there are other recommendations regarding this person's involvement in the internship. For example, the person who works with aspiring administrators at this point in their career development has a very special opportunity to work in ways that are quite important for each intern. Advise on how to handle issues faced in the field or how to work effectively with a mentor administrator who might not share the same views as the intern. is often sought. Long-range job searching is frequently something with which a supervisor may be helpful. These and many other activities of the interns' supervisor carry with them a continuing responsibility to be available and open to work with interns.

If you are a university supervisor, in what ways do you make yourself available to the interns with whom you work? (E-mail? Additional site visits? Required one-to-one conferencing?)

_____

_____

_____

_____

_____

_____

_____

_____

Summary

In this chapter, suggestions were offered regarding the ways in which the role of the university faculty member responsible for supervising or coordinating an administrative internship may be assisted in carrying out this duty. We started by noting how important the use of periodic seminars involving all administrative interns each term are for the benefit of those who wish to become school leaders. It was noted that such sessions are useful ways to introduce information to groups who share common interests and concerns about their work as administrators. It was also noted that an important outcome of internship seminars may also be the creation of a greater sense of collegiality among those who will soon be administrators in the field.

Next, we considered the broad responsibilities of anyone who serves to coordinate an internship. It was noted that the supervisor or coordinator is responsible for knowing university requirements and procedures, the expectations of the state education agency, and most important, the needs and interests of those serving as interns.

The chapter concludes with a review of some of the major "job description" duties that need to be addressed by anyone serving as the coordinator of the intern program at a university. It was noted that, in large measure, the ways in which these duties are carried out has a lot to do with the extent to which the individual university faculty members commit themselves to service on a continuing basis to the future leaders with whom they work.

CHAPTER 7

The Field Mentor

From the Field 7.1

When he was going through the administrator certification program at Piney Tree University a few years ago, Frank Dunlap promised himself that when he became a principal he would do whatever he could do to help local educators who wanted to move into school administration in the future. He remembered the classes at Piney Tree where local principals and assistant principals came in as members of guest panels to talk about the "real world" of school administration. He recalled the class in Educational Finance where Dr. Stuart Carmody served as the instructor for a quarter. Dr. Carmody was the Chief Financial Officer for the county, and he really knew about the way to manage money in schools. Most of all, Frank remembered the great experience while he was completing the internship required for certification. He worked with his own principal, Lucius Washington, as his mentor during that term, and he suddenly saw how all the "parts" of administration that he had learned in classes fit together on a daily basis. Frank often smiles when he thinks of how well these kinds of experiences help him now that he is the principal of Western Middle School.

Frank was really pleased that two of his teachers were now enrolled in the Piney Tree Principal Preparation Program. He was glad because he knew that soon both of these individuals would be coming to him to ask if they could carry out their internships under his direction here at Western. He could now be a contributor in the way Mr. Washington was a few years ago. But now that this opportunity was on his doorstep, he began to wonder about the ways in which he could meet the new challenge. What was he supposed to do, now that he was a mentor?

Perhaps one of the most complex issues associated with the internship experienced used in the preservice preparation of school administrators is that it truly requires a great deal of cooperation among many different parties. The intern, for example, must invest a great deal of personal time and effort engaging in the type of learning activities that ensure the quality of the intern experience. In addition, a positive relationship needs to be formed with the university supervisor if the internship is to be effective. Also, as we noted in the previous chapter, the university supervisor or coordinator has a great amount of control over whether the internship will be a positive experience. Not only does he or she have to respond effectively to the needs of the interns, but the supervisor must also provide a conceptual or academic framework in which "learning by doing" may be grounded and cast as a positive experience.

The third member of the "learning team" that contributes to the effectiveness of the internship is, of course, the practicing administrator (or administrators) who work in the field on a regular basis with the aspiring principal or assistant principal. This chapter is directed toward presenting a description of the role and responsibilities associated with those who take on the critical role of assisting colleagues to acquire the skills and knowledge associated with instructional leadership. We begin by noting some of the desired characteristics that would be demonstrated by an individual who works with interns in the field. Next, we describe some of the basic responsibilities associated with effective mentoring for aspiring school leaders. Finally, we look at the ways in which successful collaboration may occur among the intern, the university supervisor, and the persons who serve as field mentors. Throughout, we invite your reflection on various elements of these descriptions as you prepare for your own internship or as you continue with your own field-based learning experiences.

Characteristics of Effective Field Mentors

Traditionally, those who would serve as mentors have been identified quite simply as expert practitioners in some field. In addition, mentors have also been described as individuals with many more years of experience working in a particular field than their mentees or protégés. As a result, when many people think of a "mentor," they often think of someone who is older, more experienced, and in many cases, nearing the end of his or her career and willing to pass wisdom and experiences on to those beginning the same profession.

Before going any farther with research-based descriptions of effective mentor characteristics, it may be wise for you to reflect on some of the individuals who have already mentored you in your personal or professional life. After all, probably none of us would be where we are today if we had not had important influence us in significant ways over the years.

List some of the people who have mentored you in your life. After each name, write a brief description of how that person influenced you in a positive way.

Now, see how these people match some of the following characteristics, which have been identified in the literature and research related to people who are effective mentors to aspiring and beginning school administrators.

1. Effective mentors should have experience as practicing school administrators, and they should be regarded by peers and others as effective.

2. Effective mentors must demonstrate generally accepted positive leadership qualities, such as (but not limited to) the following:
   a. intelligence
   b. good oral and written communication skills
   c. past, present, and future understanding with simultaneous orientation
   d. acceptance of multiple alternative solutions to complex problems
   e. clarity of vision and the ability to share that vision with others in the organization

3. Mentors need to be able to ask the right questions of aspiring administrators and interns and not just provide the "right" answers all the time.

4. Effective mentors must accept an alternative way of doing things and avoid the tendency to tell beginners that the way to do things is "the way I used to do it."

5. Effective mentors should express a desire to see people go beyond their present levels of performance, even if that might mean that their protégés are able to do some things better than the mentors can.

6. Effective mentors need to model the principles of continuous learning and reflection.

7. Effective mentors must exhibit an awareness of the political and social realities of life in at least one school system; they must know the "real ways" that things get done.

As you reflect on your own career as an educator, you might consider how these characteristics fit the mentors you have known.

In addition to the characteristics of effective mentors noted above, other skills and abilities are often used to describe "ideal mentors." Typically, these individuals demonstrate:

- Knowledge, skills, and expertise in a particular field of practice
- Enthusiasm that is sincere and convincing, and most important, the ability to convey this feeling to those they are mentoring
- The ability to communicate to others a clear picture of personal attitudes, values, and ethical standards
- The ability to communicate in a sensitive way the type of feedback needed regarding another person's progress toward goals, standards, competence, and professional behavior
- The ability to listen to colleagues' ideas, doubts, concerns, and questions
- A caring attitude, a belief in their colleagues' potential flexibility, and a sense of humor

In cases where you may have a chance to select a specific administrator with whom you will carry out your internship experience, these criteria may be helpful. Regardless of whether potential mentors possess all of the above characteristics, anyone who would serve as an administrative mentor to you as an intern should be willing to address the five following important skills as part of working with you and other interns:

1. They must have a willingness to invest time and energy in the professional development of their colleagues.
2. They must have a strong conviction and belief that other administrators are likely to have a positive effect on the quality of schooling.
3. They must have confidence in their own abilities.
4. They must possess high standards and expectations of their own abilities and of the work of their colleagues.
5. They must believe that mentoring is a mutually enhancing professional development opportunity in which both partners will achieve equal satisfaction from the relationship.

As you read over the lists on the last few pages, you will no doubt begin to wonder if the expectations of the person with whom you will work during your internship are set too high. After all, in most cases, you will not have an opportunity to go through an elaborate selection process to determine who will be your field mentor during the internship. In the majority of programs across the nation, internships are carried out in the schools in which the interns are normally employed. Few school systems provide aspiring administrators with released time from their classroom or other duties to go through the kinds of intensive, full-time internships that might be desirable. Simply stated, the person who might serve as your field mentor might present anything but the kinds of behaviors you wish to follow in your professional life. But, because of circumstances you cannot control, you have no choice. Nevertheless, even in situations where you must work with a less-than-perfect mentor, we believe that it is likely that some of the characteristics noted earlier in this section might be available to you.

If you know who your administrator field mentor will be for the internship, use the space below to identify the most positive features of his or her work as a leader, something that you believe you can acquire during this field experience. Focus on the positives, not the limitations.

_____

_____

_____

_____

_____

_____

_____

_____

Finally, remember that there will be opportunities to observe and work with more than one administrator while carrying out your internship. Even if the person who is your primary field mentor is not "perfect" with regard to the "Characteristics of Effective Mentors," it is possible to learn from the many different people you will encounter.

Responsibilities of Field Mentors

Now that we have reviewed some of the characteristics of effective mentors for interns, let us look at some of their major duties and responsibilities.

Among the major responsibilities of administrator field mentors working with interns are:

- Giving their time to interns
- Listening to and sympathizing with interns without necessarily condoning or condemning what may at times seem to be inappropriate or ineffective actions

- Manifesting a sense of humor, but also avoiding sarcasm and cynicism
- Appreciating that good leaders are sometimes not able to play the role of effective mentors, but that effective mentors must always be good leaders

In concrete terms, the field mentor is responsible for letting the intern see which duties will be a part of the job of serving as a future school administrator. In addition, the mentor needs to present an open and honest picture of what life will be like when the intern sits in the "hot seat" of the principal or assistant principal for the first time. Here are some suggested activities for the field mentor to carry out with his or her interns as a way to address the first goal, namely helping interns understand the official job of being an administrator.

Set Goals and Objectives

No doubt, certain objectives have been specified for every intern engaged in this learning activity. These objectives may have been set by the state education agency, the university, or through some form of blending both interest groups. Further, as we noted in earlier chapters, we assume that each intern has also established a set of personal learning objectives to be achieved as a result of this field experience.

Regardless of all the other goal statements and objectives that may have been established prior to this time, it is still important for the field supervisor and intern to engage in a one-to-one development of the specific goals and objectives that are to be achieved as a result of their interaction. Goals set by the state department may lead a person toward developing general administrative competence. However, when an intern works next to an experienced administrator for a lengthy period of time, the assumption might be made that, because of the unique personalities, skills, and interests of the intern and mentor, additional goals and objectives may be set. For example, an intern may be working with an individual who has particular strengths in curriculum development, or perhaps student discipline. As a result, the intern may wish to identify certain target areas for personal learning that extend beyond minimal standards and relate to the learning resource now available.

In the space below, identify any specific goals and objectives that may be appropriate for an intern working in this setting with this particular mentor administrator in the field.

_____

_____

_____

_____

_____

_____

_____

_____

Meet at Least Weekly to Describe What Regular, Predictable Duties Face the Administrator in the Next Few Days

A big part of being an administrator, of course, involves being able to react to situations that occur without warning. A fight breaks out between students in a hallway, a bomb threat occurs, a parent needs "just a few minutes of your time," and so forth. No amount of discussion and prior planning between the mentor and intern can prepare for these unplanned events. However, there are many things that can be predicted and prepared for as a school term progresses. These include such things as getting ready for staff development days, report card conferencing, state and school district inventories and other reports, and so forth. For events like these, experienced administrators have typically developed at least a mental checklist of who to contact, what materials have to be prepared, whether memos need to be sent out, whether rooms need to be reserved, whether work orders must be sent to building or district custodial staff, and many similar concerns. Interns can learn a lot about their future duties by being a part of this work flow and, in some cases, can be delegated the duty of actually carrying out some of this work. For example, if local policy dictates an annual inventory of all audiovisual equipment in a building, the intern can be assigned the duty of ensuring that this task gets done. (By the way, that does not necessarily mean that the intern goes around and actually counts overhead projectors!)

There are also other times during a school year when experienced field mentors can alert their interns to probable events that are not on the calendar of official due dates. For example, experienced high school principals may have a very keen sense of when 12th graders are planning a "Senior Skip Day" and begin to take steps to alert students, parents, and teachers to official policies that might prohibit such events. A field mentor can also predict for an intern the periods of time in which he or she might experience a higher-than-average number of parents requesting appointments.

As you think about the school year, list some of the important events (either formal or informal) that need to be addressed at predictable times, and that should serve as the basis of discussions between mentor and intern.

Be Candid and Open

There are many things that a principal must deal with during the course of a day that must remain confidential. While it is critical that interns see the real world of administration as much as possible, there are some things that the principal cannot share. Matters of staff personnel, student records, and many conversations must be kept as closed matters, even to the most trustworthy of interns. We recommend that, at the beginning of the internship, the field mentor and intern have a frank conversation about this issue and develop an understanding of the fact that, without explanation, the mentor might need to ask an intern to leave the office, stay away from certain files, or generally avoid matters that do not allow review by anyone but the building administrator. This should not be a surprise to the intern, and certainly no offense would be intended. Discussing such matters openly and candidly is a critical aspect of the sharing that must go on.

On a different level, there are times when the intern can be brought into discussions and reflections with the principal concerning matters that may be appropriate for sharing with someone who wants to be a principal in the future. In some cases, dependent on the judgment of the mentor, discussions might occur about staff evaluation, or even how certain student discipline problems might best be handled. The mentor cannot necessarily speak openly about every matter, but at the same time, if an intern really wants to understand a job, he or she must be involved in some sensitive conversations and discussions from time to time. It is all going to be a part of the job some day.

We cannot list which things should be open to discussion and which should remain closed and confidential under all circumstances in all settings; this is another matter that needs to be considered in the initial planning of an internship in any school. In the space below, you may wish to draft some ground rules to guide discussions and observations.

_____

_____

_____

_____

_____

_____

_____

Involve the Intern as Part of the Team

Although it would be great if all administrative interns could have full release from their normal teaching duties so they could work as full-time administrators in schools other than their own, that is not the way in which most people proceed through field experiences. In the majority of principal preparation programs, engaging in an internship is an activity added to a person's normal work duties. Teachers who want to be principals spend most of their workday in their classrooms and, where possible, find time to work with their field mentor principals and carry out administrative activities on the side.

Even in this type of part-time experience, interns need to have contact with their administrative mentors. They also need to get the feel of the world of school administration by having access to materials, information, records, and other resources that would be open to them if they were principals or assistant principals. Unfortunately, in a school where a person is known as only "one of the teachers," such access is often denied by staff. Even more problematic are cases where interns cannot visit with their mentor administrator on a regular basis because secretaries and clerks "protect" principals from other staff members.

A way to avoid these problems could begin with the mentor administrator making certain to introduce the intern to key staff members at the beginning of the term in which the intern will work in the building. It is important that the principal's secretary, chief custodian, cafeteria manager, and other key staff members recognize that a teacher is learning a new educational role. Therefore the intern must be seen in a different light than when he or she would come into the main office, cafeteria, or other areas of the school as one of the teachers. Specifically, the mentor administrator must make it clear to all that the intern needs to be able to have contact with the administrator at times when others might be kept away from the office door.

The mentor administrator also needs to ensure that other teachers are aware that one of their colleagues is serving as an intern, and that one of the ways this will be successful is by learning how to work with teachers in a way other than as a peer. This in no way means that other teachers should suddenly be instructed to obey the intern or to defer to him or her. Rather, they need to be alerted to the fact that, in some cases, they may find the intern in the main office, and not the principal or assistant principal. The mentor can begin to help this process along by doing some small things, like asking the intern to do the morning announcements, go around the building with visitors, or attend department or team meetings from time to time, if these activities are normally carried out only by the principal or assistant principal. In short, an important part of learning how to be an administrator is to begin to understand how it feels to have others look at you in a different light. It is also critical that an intern be able to have the freedom to move about the building in the way that he or she would if actually an administrator.

In the space below, write down some specific ways in which the intern might be made more visible in the school as a member of the leadership team.

_____

_____

_____

_____

_____

_____

_____

_____

Showcase the Intern

As we noted in Chapter 2, one of the potential benefits of an internship is that interns can use this learning experience as a way to market and demonstrate their talents as future administrators. As a result, an important practice for administrator field mentors is to make certain that interns may be seen by other administrative colleagues from time to time. For example, one activity that may be helpful in this regard would be bringing an intern along to one or more district principals' meetings. Or, the intern may be asked to represent a school at a meeting normally attended by principals or assistant principals. It may be possible to find a committee where an intern may be a good contributor to the issues being reviewed. No matter what strategy is employed, it is very helpful for an intern to have the opportunity to interact with others in a district who may at some point be influential to an individual seeking an administrative appointment in the future.

Indicate any ways that may be appropriate for you to make the talents of an intern noticed by other administrators.

Assess Performance

Whether it is required in the role of the field mentor by the local university or not, another critical duty involves the assessment of the intern's performance. Simply stated, the question is whether or not, in the judgment of an experienced school administrator who served as a mentor, the intern performed well enough to warrant consideration as a serious candidate for an assistant principalship or principalship in the near future. This type of assessment can come in several forms. One may be as part of a formal intern evaluation process requested by the intern's institution. A second may be in the form of an exit interview with the intern, a practice being employed in many cases across the nation. Yet another way in which the assessment process might take place is by providing a letter of reference for an individual who has worked with the experienced administrator. This type of assessment, regardless of form, might be quite difficult to complete, particularly if an intern did not do a particularly effective job. On the other hand, honest feedback can ultimately be one of the most valuable things that an aspiring administrator might receive while completing a field experience.

In the space below, provide a brief description of the way in which you intend to evaluate an intern with whom you may be working.

_____

_____

_____

The list of responsibilities noted here is not meant to be an exhaustive statement of everything that a field mentor should or might do with interns. The mentor may choose to go beyond these suggested activities, or there may be additional requirements specified by the state department of education, the local university, or the school district. Our goal here has been to alert mentors that there is much to their duties in terms of helping future colleagues grow professionally. It is not simply enough to "fill out a few forms and let an intern hang around the main office and run some errands for a semester."

Collaboration Is the Key

Throughout this chapter, we have suggested that the field mentor administrator has a number of specific duties that he or she must carry out when working with interns from a local university. It may have appeared as if these duties were easily assigned to only a single person such as the principal or assistant principal in a local school who agrees to work with an aspiring administrator enrolled in a class. The fact of the matter is that the work of the field mentor is only one part of a complex set of relationships that need to be formed as one way to support a very important learning process. The field mentor must work effectively with the university supervisor, and, most important, there must be an effective collaborative partnership formed between the field mentor and the intern.

As we noted in Chapter 6, the university supervisor or coordinator of administrative internships has a number of responsibilities that include planning the internships, arranging for appropriate field sites, visiting interns, conducting periodic seminars, and, finally, evaluating the internships according to the standards established by the university and the state department of education. There is also a critical need for the supervisor to maintain effective and open relationships with field mentors, as well. Both of these parties must engage in frequent conversations about the progress of interns in the field. The field mentor cannot afford to have wholly inept individuals working as interns in a school. On the other hand, the university supervisor can ill afford to have individuals who are not ready to profit from the internship because they have failed to get a solid grounding at the university. Both situations will likely eventually result in a loss of confidence between two key partners in the internship process.

Finally, the intern must take a great deal of the responsibility for creating an effective partnership with the field mentor. At minimum, the intern must do the work assigned by the mentor. More than that, however, the intern has a responsibility to maintain effective communication with the mentor so that the mentor can have an understanding of the progress being made. In some unfortunate cases, interns accept an assignment with a particular principal, yet spend an inordinate amount of time grumbling about what they are not getting from their field mentor. In the real world of school administration, grumbling about problems does not solve anything. Communication and dialogue are the only responsible approaches to dealing with issues of concern.

Summary

In this chapter, we covered a number of issues associated with the role of the field mentor administrator who will work with interns during a semester or quarter. We began by noting the characteristics of effective administrative mentors who have worked in programs across the country with either aspiring or beginning administrators. While we realize that, in most cases, interns will rarely have the opportunity to go through a lengthy process of selecting the "perfect" mentor, there is value in looking at some of the features that might be demonstrated by mentors. Interns can then seek these behaviors as they proceed through their field experience.

Next, we considered some of the specific activities and responsibilities that might be expected of field mentors who work with interns. Several specific activities were suggested as ways of helping interns, and we also noted that other practices might be developed in different cases.

Finally, we noted that the best internships are not simply something done by one or two people. Instead, the most profitable forms of field-based learning require a constant spirit of collaboration among the intern, the university supervisor, and of course, the field mentor.

CHAPTER 8

The Role of the Intern

From the Field 8.1

Amy Brady was in a euphoric frame of mind. For the past 3 years she had been attending Ascot University as a school administration major. During her course of study she had taken 30 credits of work in the theory and practice of educational leadership. Now she was ready to try her hand at real leadership. For the next full academic year she would be serving as an administrative intern in her school district.

Prior to the beginning of the new academic year, Amy touched all the bases necessary to prepare for her internship experience. She first met with university officials to gain an understanding of the university's internship requirements. Next, she met with the superintendent of her school district and the principal of her building (who would be her field mentor) to discuss the university's requirements and how they coordinated with the district's ability to facilitate her internship program. Finally, she began to conduct preplanning activities with colleagues to prepare for the impending projects that would constitute her administrative internship.

But even with all this preparation, Amy still experienced moments of apprehension about her success in the internship. She began to think she would not have enough time to do all the required work. She was concerned about how her colleagues would react toward her as an administrative intern. Would they be willing to help her when she asked? After all, as an administrative intern she could easily be viewed as part of the building leadership, and for some of her colleagues that meant she was "different." But her major concern was wondering exactly what she had to do to be a successful intern. She felt her role in this endeavor was designed by and for others rather than herself. While she was well informed about what she was expected to do, she was very apprehensive about how to go about doing it. Thus, she queries, "What must I do to meet the requirements of a successful internship experience?"

Amy is not alone with her feelings. Almost all administrative interns feel some level of unpreparedness for their field experiences. In many instances, interns feel as if they are ready at the knowledge level, but fall short at the "doing" level. This is only natural. For most, 100% of their time has been spent in the classroom learning theory and discussing its application.

Who are the university officials you must meet with to determine your internship requirements?

_____

_____

_____

Who are the school district and building officials you must meet with to determine how site personnel will facilitate your internship?

_____

_____

_____

Who are the staff personnel you must meet with to discuss predetermined projects and/or preplanning activities?

_____

_____

_____

_____

What predetermined projects and/or preplanning activities can you discuss with staff personnel?

_____

_____

_____

_____

In order to be a successful intern, you must be able to enact three specific roles. You should be prepared to be (a) a willing learner; (b) a partner with your field colleagues and university mentor; and (c) a reflective practitioner.

The Intern as Learner

During your internship, you must commit yourself to being a *willing learner*. This means you must come to work each day with an inquisitive mind. You must seek to gain a total understanding of the intellectual challenges you will be confronted with at your internship site. You must put your position in the proper perspective. Your recent university classroom experiences have provided you with only a part of what you must know in order to be an effective school administrator.

Your internship is an extraordinary opportunity for you to test your classroom knowledge before you actually accept the responsibilities of a real job situation. This is a time for you to be open-minded. You should challenge yourself to explore and examine all phases of a school administrator's job. You should be prepared to question the actions and behaviors of practicing administrators. You *must* continually question your own emerging administrative behavior.

As a *learner* you must be willing to commit the time, effort, and energy it takes to become an effective school leader. Some of you will have the luxury of a full-time internship. Others will have part-time assignments. Still others will have to work full-time jobs and tailor their internship activities around their professional obligations. It does not matter what time configuration you must comply with, a meaningful internship is a time-consuming, labor-intensive undertaking. You must deal with your circumstances. They will challenge your ability to enhance and extend your leadership skills.

One of the major intellectual challenges you will face as an intern will be to learn the culture of the school building to which you are assigned. You will find yourself in one of four types of situations when it comes to learning the school building's culture.

1. *You have been a teaching staff member in the building.* In this situation it is very likely that you will have a good understanding of the building's organizational culture. You will be familiar with the stakeholders, influential staff members, and the impact of parents and community organizations and their values and belief systems. But remember, your perspective of that culture is from a staff position, not from an administrative one. Administrators and teachers often do not see every characteristic of their building culture from the same point of view. It will be important for you to learn to understand how administrators view the organizational culture, as well as how it influences their decision making. These insights will also give you an opportunity to develop your own decision-making posture.

2. *You already hold some administrative position in the building* (e.g., director of guidance, department supervisor, or athletic director). This situa-

tion certainly will give you a great advantage in learning how the culture affects other administrator's leadership roles and decision-making strategies. You may feel that you already know everything about the culture from this perspective. Remember that you are studying to be a principal. You have not experienced how a building culture impacts the role of a principal, so do not make assumptions and you will learn more from your internship experience.

3. *Your internship site is in the district in which you work, but in another building.* In this situation, you will more than likely have some idea of how the district culture operates in the building. However, you will have to explore how the building administration and staff uniquely respond to the district culture. In addition, you will have to discern the building's own culture.

4. *Your internship site is in a different district than the one in which you practice.* In this situation, the cultural learning curve will be at its steepest. You will have to investigate the entire organization to determine the type of culture that exists and how it impacts the roles of administrators. You will have to learn about stakeholders, veteran influencers, values, and belief systems. In effect, you will be facing an unknown situation as you begin to learn the entire culture.

What unique cultural characteristics do you already know about your internship site?

_____

_____

_____

_____

_____

_____

How might these characteristics influence building administrators' leadership styles and decision making?

_____

_____

_____

_____

_____

How might these characteristics influence your leadership style and decision making?

_____

_____

_____

_____

_____

_____

Another challenge that will require you to be a willing learner is that you must understand all of the government and district rules and regulations that guide the leadership and management of the building. You must remember that schools are compliance institutions. Most of the work conducted in a school building takes place because it is mandated by law. Many times, a leader's treatment of students, staff, and parents is guided by district policy. You must know these policies. You must be aware of how to apply them. In many situations you must be able to apply them very quickly. You will have very little room for error in the application of these policies. The consequences of not knowing how government rules and regulations are applied at a building site could be costly to the district, your job, or both.

What are the most important policies that you should know about at your internship site?

_____

_____

_____

_____

_____

_____

You may feel as though you know a lot of theory about leadership and what leaders do, but there is much more to learn outside the university classroom. Remember that even in the best degree programs it is difficult to simulate reality in a pure laboratory environment. When you begin your internship you will be replacing classroom learning with "learning by doing." You will actually experience the role of a building leader. Your intern responsibilities and duties will be to enact the role of a school administrator. You will be required to translate theory into practice. You will be required to make decisions about leadership styles and strategies. You will be required to organize and motivate staff members to work on special projects. You will be required to handle student discipline problems. You will be required to interact with parents and community residents. Remember, you will not be discussing the theory of how you should do these things—you will actually be doing them.

What specific "learning by doing" characteristics can you attribute to your internship?

_____

_____

_____

_____

_____

_____

The Intern as Partner

The organizational structure of your internship should be a partnership among yourself, your field mentor, and your university mentor. This partnership should be founded on a vision and set of goals that describe what you must accomplish by the end of your experience. Before you even begin your internship experience, a mutually developed, written understanding of the exact parameters that will shape that experience should exist. This agreement will help ensure the success of your internship.

The agreement should clearly describe the specific expectations that both parties will have of you. For example, it is one thing for the university to require that you exhibit leadership behavior while you are performing your internship duties, but it is another thing for the administrators at your internship site to delegate any kind of responsibility that would require such behavior. Thus, it is important to define specific activities that will provide you with an opportunity to develop your leadership skills.

From the Field 8.2

It is not unusual for school districts to be a bit squeamish about letting an intern function in a "real" leadership capacity. District or government policies and regulations often prohibit that anyone but a certified administrator do a specific job (e.g., officially observing a teacher's performance). However, it is possible for interns to do some administrative work without fear of compromising the law. For example, any type of student discipline (except a suspension or an expulsion), talking to dis-enchanted parents, or leading a staff project to effect a program change are all ac-ceptable activities. There is also the possibility of simulating experience. For exam-ple, with a teacher's permission an intern could observe a class. Of course, the observation would not be official. However, the intern and the teacher could role play the entire observation process. This would give the intern some feeling for what it is like to conduct this activity. This is the type of information that should be an integral part of the intern-mentor partnership agreement.

Another important aspect of your partnership with your mentors has to do with matching the expectations that you have of yourself with the expecta-tions that they have of you. These expectations should be symbiotic. In addi-tion, they should be high-level expectations, so your work will be meaningful to your future practice.

When expectations are not mutual, there is a potential for conflict be-tween you and your mentors. If it is unclear what is expected of you, you will find it very difficult to identify viable activities for your participation. This will not help you in your endeavor to become an effective school administrator.

What are the five most important expectations that you hold for yourself as an administrative intern?

_____

_____

_____

_____

_____

What are the five most important expectations that your university men-tor has of you?

_____

_____

_____

_____

_____

What are the five most important expectations that your field mentor has of you?

_____

_____

_____

_____

_____

_____

What are the major similarities and differences between the expectations that are held of you by your mentor and those you hold for yourself?

_____

_____

_____

_____

_____

_____

The Intern as Reflective Practitioner

One of the major lessons you will have to learn as an intern is how effective school administrators should function as reflective practitioners. Building leaders make many decisions that affect the lives of many different people. Any one of their decisions could affect staff, students, and parents all at the same time and all differently. There never seems to be a time when everyone is satisfied with a decision. To paraphrase an old Lincoln quote, "You can [satisfy] all of the people some of the time. And, you can [satisfy] some of the people all of the time. But, you can't [satisfy] all of the people all of the time." There will be times when your decisions will be accepted by one faction and rejected by others. There will also be times when you will have to enforce compliance with decisions. Government laws and regulations and/or board of education policy drive these decisions. Even though these decisions protect your building and district from violating the law, some individuals will protest their implementation and expect you to help them circumvent the requirement. To prepare for situations like this, you should have a way of assessing your decisions and decision-making process.

You must understand that all your decisions, whether or not they are driven by policy, are quite often affected by your own personal values and belief systems. Furthermore, you must understand that those who differ with your decisions are doing so from the perspective of their own values and beliefs. Effective school administrators monitor their responses and evaluate the responses of others by developing a strong sense of self-awareness through the use of reflective practice. *Reflective practice* is defined as "a means by which [you] can develop a greater self-awareness about the nature and impact of [your] performance" (Osterman & Kottkamp, 1993). By using reflective practice you will be able to revisit your decisions and continually measure their impact on others. In addition, reflective practice will help you match your actions and behavior to your personal values and belief systems.

The "way to review one's personal value and belief systems as they may be related to the realities of [an internship] is through a periodic review of something called a personal educational platform" (Daresh & Playko, 1997). This statement clearly and articulately describes the beliefs related to educational issues that you hold as foundational to the definition of your work life. This platform is constructed of "planks" that are nonnegotiable values representing core beliefs related to your job. In effect, a platform is a statement that describes you as a professional educator. It serves as a guide for you to measure such things as the parameters of a job offer, the performance requirements of a position, or the way you believe you are being perceived by others.

Constructing a Platform for Your Internship Experience

There are many ways for a person to design a personal educational platform. We do not pay homage to any one in particular. However, there are a series of questions that you should reflect on and answer in some detail before you start to craft your platform in earnest. These questions reflect some of the important core issues that you will be confronted with as an administrative intern. They do not reflect all of the questions that might be answered for such an exercise, nor do they appear in any order of priority or importance. They are all of equal importance. We invite you to add to this list any questions that you feel are important to internships in general or to your unique internship situation.

1. *What is my purpose in this undertaking?* The number of answers to this question could equal the number of interns going through the experience. Is this just another hoop that you must jump through to get your degree? Is it truly an opportunity for you to practice your leadership skills? Is it the beginning of the process of your becoming an effective school administrator? Do you know any other purposes? Indicate them in the space provided below.

_____

_____

_____

_____

_____

2. *What are the key ingredients of a successful internship experience?* You must consider an answer to this question before you begin your internship. Whatever answer you come up with should be a driving force for determining the types of activities and projects that you should be experiencing. It should also be used as a guide for informing the officials at your internship site what you expect them to do to facilitate your effort.

_____

_____

_____

_____

_____

3. *What are the fundamental leadership theories that will influence my behavior?* What fundamental leadership theory or theories do you hold? How do you expect them to influence your behavior in your internship? What leadership styles do you anticipate experimenting with during your internship? What leadership strategies do you anticipate using?

_____

_____

_____

_____

_____

4. *What are the fundamental change agent theories that will influence my behavior?* More than likely, you will be involved in some project that will require you to facilitate program change or organizational change. This will not be an easy task. What are your beliefs when it comes to bringing about change in a school building?

How do you approach voluntary change? What if the state government mandates a change? How do you approach mandated change as opposed to voluntary change?

_____

_____

_____

_____

_____

5. *How do my espoused theories relate to theories in practice?* You are going to find that there is a degree of difficulty in practicing what you preach. Many times it is not your fault. Education is a highly regulated service. There are many noneducators who have a final say in what happens in schools (e.g., legislators, judges, and board of education members). Sometimes, their dicta will not match what you believe as a professional. There will be times when you voluntarily make a decision that will not seem to match what you preach to your faculty. Is it important to practice your espoused theories? What can you do if an authoritative body tells you to enforce a practice that is antithetical to your espoused theories? What do you do if you purposefully defy one of your espoused theories?

_____

_____

_____

_____

_____

6. *How will I know if I am learning to be an effective school administrator?* You must continually seek feedback from your field mentor and your university mentor. Both these individuals should be able to discuss how well you are proceeding toward your appointed objectives. How do you characterize an effective school administrator? What types of activities do you need to participate in to practice how to be an effective school administrator?

_____

_____

_____

_____

_____

_____

7. *How do I want students to view me during my internship experience?* When you become an administrator, even as an intern, students view you differently. If you have anything to do with discipline, they accord you an appropriate title to go along with your particular discipline style. No matter what, they probably will not view you as you would want to be viewed. It is a good exercise for you to imagine how you want them to view you and what you may have to do to help them see you from your perspective.

_____

_____

_____

_____

_____

8. *How do I want my teaching colleagues to view me during my internship experience?* Upon completion of your internship, if you walked up to one of your teaching colleagues and asked him or her to reflect on your behavior and decorum as an intern, what would you want to hear? How do you want to be perceived as an administrator? How do you want to be perceived as a leader?

_____

_____

_____

_____

_____

9. *What are my nonnegotiable values for this internship?* This question is extremely important. It addresses the issues that are most dear to you as an educator. If for some reason you feel that these issues are not in compliance with these values, you could easily decide that school administration is not for you.

_____

_____

_____

_____

_____

_____

On Being a Reflective Intern

Experimenting with reflective practice will be time-consuming. During your internship, however, it is extremely important for you to do it. It will have a profound effect on the final outcome of your internship experience. If you do it correctly, you will be able to make very wise decisions about your future in school administration. You will also have an excellent beginning for an actual practice as a school administrator.

There are many different ways to conduct reflective practice. We do not endorse any particular one. However, we believe that there are two extremely important activities that you must participate in if you are to benefit from the practice: (a) developing a platform and (b) using an interactive-reflective journal.

1. *You should develop a platform document.* You should develop a clear, articulate statement that reflects the answers to questions like those cited in the previous pages of this chapter. This should not be a statement that you develop just for your internship. You should approach the crafting of the statement as though it represented one that you would write for a real job situation. This statement can serve you in several ways: (a) It will provide you with an opportunity to articulate your position as a professional educator; (b) it will provide you with a vehicle for communicating your educational philosophy to your colleagues; and (c) it will help chart a plan for your future professional development.

In the space provided below, list the planks of your personal educational platform for your administrative internship.

_____

_____

_____

_____

_____

_____

_____

_____

_____

_____

_____

_____

_____

Now begin to craft a platform statement from the planks you cited above.

_____

_____

_____

_____

_____

_____

_____

_____

_____

_____

_____

_____

_____

Remember that your personal vision statement is a "work in progress." It can be used during your internship to guide you and to show others where you stand on major educational issues and problems. It represents your current thinking. Every time you modify your thoughts about an educational issue, you should revisit your personal vision statement. It should be kept current on at least an annual basis.

2. *You should use an interactive-reflective journal as a data collection instrument.* You should have some instrument for documenting your thoughts about your internship experience. In doing so, it is essential that you commit your impressions to hard copy as quickly as possible. We suggest that you set aside a period of time each week (at a minimum) to sit and reflect on the events of a specific period of time. It is best to do this when you can spend some quality time alone. Your interactive-reflective journal should include your impressions of such items as the following:

- Your leadership performance at a specific event (e.g., staff meeting, committee meeting)

- The reactions of others to your leadership performance at a specific event (sometimes this information is not readily discernible because people will mask their honest opinions; however, you should document whatever you observe)

- The leadership ability of others at a specific event (e.g., the principal's leadership ability at a staff meeting)

- The reactions of others regarding the leadership ability of building administration at a specific event

- Your decision-making ability

- The decision-making ability of others

- The general staff morale in the building

- The nature and condition of the organizational culture

- General student attitude and behavior

These items represent only a portion of the data that you can reflect upon. It would be impossible for us to list them all. However, these illustrations should give you a good idea as to the type of material you should consider for reflection. Essentially, the journal becomes your personal diary. It is your opportunity to make personal statements about your leadership ability, the perceived leadership abilities of others, the culture and climate of the building, what is happening in and to the education profession, and so on.

Your effort to capture these data should be done in a consistent format. We suggest that you use an instrument that will permit you to organize information so you can use it later for research. The following illustrates how you can set up an interactive-reflective journal.

1. Divide a sheet of paper in half by scoring a line about halfway from the left-hand margin.

2. Label the left section "Activity Facts."

3. Label the right section "Reflections." (see Figure 8.1)

Under the section labeled "Activity Facts" indicate the nature of the activity, such as staff meeting (January 11, 2000), committee meeting (March 3, 2000), and so on. If an agenda was used, you can either attach it to the journal or indicate the agenda items under "Activity Facts." Under the section labeled "Reflections" write your thoughts regarding the facts. The content in the "Reflections" section will obviously be longer than the content in the "Activity Facts" section. If you are committed to keeping the journal as we suggest, ultimately you will have a detailed accounting of your internship experience.

Figure 8.1. Example of an Interactive-Reflective Journal

Activity Facts	*Reflections*
1/11/2000 Staff Meeting Discuss new report card format	The staff seems to want a new report card format but does not want it to be more complex than the one in current use. The principal showed her willingness to work with them, but I don't believe they really want to do anything this year. The item was tabled. The principal really illustrated effective leadership here. She was extremely patient and did not try to force the staff to accept her way (even though she believes the report card should be changed immediately).
Announced the need for a new committee to restructure the building discipline policy	Mrs. Bundy asked staff members to volunteer to serve on a discipline policy committee. She indicated that I would be the chairperson for the committee. I like the fact that she let faculty volunteer, rather than appointing members. This way those staff members on the committee will tend to be more favorable to the "mountain" of work we have ahead of us.
Staff questions and concerns	
3/2/2000 Science Curriculum Committee Meeting	
Personal reflections	This is my first try at leading a group of faculty member in a project effort. I have to remember that their initial willingness to listen to everything I have to say is their reaction to my internship position, not my leadership ability. I hope that will come later!
Agenda Items	

Figure 8.2. Sample Agreement for the Administrative Internship

The Intern _____ [name], whose address is _____ and whose telephone number is _____, has voluntarily enrolled in the Master of Arts Degree program in the College of Education at _____ University. The Intern's Mentor at the University is _____ [name], who can be reached at _____ [telephone number and extension].

As a condition of earning that master's degree, the Intern has agreed to participate in a field internship during the 20__-20__ school year at the _____ [school], which is located at _____ and whose telephone number is _____.

The Intern will work on the research project or projects that have been approved by the Intern's University Mentor and Field Mentor, copies of which are attached hereto as Exhibit A. The Intern, Field Mentor, and University Mentor understand that if the research project is to be modified, it will only be done so with the express written permission of the University Mentor and Field Mentor. The Intern understands that the completion of this internship and field project is part of the master's degree requirement, and that the _____ [school] is under no obligation to provide release time or additional consideration for the services provided by the Intern as part of the internship.

During the internship, the Field Mentor agrees to act as the Intern's primary supervisor. The Field Mentor also agrees to submit a written assessment of the Intern to the University Mentor at the conclusion of the internship and to meet with the University Mentor to discuss the Intern's progress at such time as both agree are appropriate. The Superintendent of Schools of _____ [school] agrees that the University Mentor may visit the school for the purposes of meeting with the Field Mentor and Intern during the course of the internship.

At the completion of the internship and as a condition of matriculating, the Intern will be required to submit such written findings or other reports as are required by the _____ University.

AGREED TO AND ACCEPTED BY

_____

[Intern]

_____

[University Mentor on behalf of College of Education]

_____

[Superintendent of Schools on behalf of school]

_____

[Field Mentor]

Summary

This chapter is designed to help you understand the role of the intern in the internship experience. A successful experience will require that you engage in three specific roles: (a) that of a willing learner, (b) that of a partner with your field and university mentors, and (c) that of a reflective practitioner. It is imperative that you seek to define how each of these roles will function in your specific internship site well in advance of your practicum. You should set up meetings with appropriate university and school-district personnel to discuss such matters. You should seek to have everything the university and your sponsoring district expect of you committed to a written agreement (see Figure 8.2 for an example).

CHAPTER 9

Evaluation and Assessment

From the Field 9.1

The academic year is winding down. Tom Hamilton is in the final weeks of his school administrative internship at Ramsville High School. For the past year, he has spent a large percentage of his extra school time performing the duties and responsibilities of a building leader. Now, he is in a countdown mode. He begins to reflect on his experiences. Two weeks ago, he led the social studies department in completing the installation of a new technology program that will help them with U.S. History I lessons. He felt really good about this project because the department had lagged behind other departments in its use of computer-assisted instruction. Now, through his help, they were excited about having the technology on hand. A few days after his work with the social studies department, he met for the last time with the Student Advisory Committee (SAC). It was his suggestion during an internship preparation meeting with the principal that initiated the SAC concept. He put together a student committee that represented Grades 9 through 12, the student council, the school newspaper, the varsity club, and the national honors society. Students elected the committee membership. This committee has met with Tom twice a month since September. The meetings focused on student concerns as well as those things that they liked about RHS. In turn, Tom shared the group's sentiments with building administration. With SAC's help, several issues that had initiated unfavorable student gossip had been attended to and remedied during the year. Last week, Tom attended his last administrative council meeting with all the district's administrators. His attendance at these meetings was very helpful in extending and enhancing his leadership skills. While he did not actively participate at all of these meetings, he was able to collect a vast amount of information about how administrators think and act while conducting their day-to-day operational tasks. He was much more sympathetic toward the job of administrator. He was even inclined to believe that the role of the high school principal was the most difficult role in school administration. He also had a better understanding of the influential impact such governing bodies as the board of education and the state legislature had on the educative process.

Yesterday, he met with the building staff for the last time as an administrative intern. When the principal announced that he had completed his tour as an administrative intern, the staff applauded for his effort and work. Tom felt very good about the staff's response. He wondered, "Does this mean that my internship was a success? How do I know if it was a success? How am I going to convince my university professors that it was a success? What do I need to assure myself that I am on the road to being an effective school administrator?"

The questions that Tom poses are not uncommon; in fact, they are very logical. After all, a number of very important people (including himself) put a great deal of time, effort, and energy into planning and implementing Tom's internship. Their effort deserves some degree of accountability data that judge Tom's work as an administrative intern. In fact, Tom's internship proposals (see Chapter 3) should have detailed how his progress as a developing leader, as well as the projects that he chose to undertake, would be evaluated during his experience.

In this chapter, we suggest some strategies for evaluating your internship experience. We will address evaluation strategies for the internship as well as your own growth as an effective school administrator.

Evaluating the Internship Experience

First, think of your internship as a total experience that included not only yourself, but also all the staff, administration, students, parents, and community members who participated in your projects. Also, consider all the individuals you had to deal with while conducting your intern duties and responsibilities. For example, discipline problems would normally include the student(s), teacher(s), and parent(s). If you were responsible for taking care of discipline problems, you were engaged in trying to facilitate the needs of all these individuals. Given this mind-set, answer the following questions about your internship.

1. *Was your internship effective?* What we are asking here is whether your internship met all of the goals and objectives as stated in the written agreement between the school district and university, as well as those cited in your project proposals.

_____

_____

_____

_____

_____

_____

In order to answer this question fully, you will have to be prepared to evaluate all the projects in which you intend to participate during your internship. Depending on the other participants, you should be prepared to use such instrumentation as: (a) pre- and postsurveys to determine the outcome of staff development training; (b) observation checklists to determine if students are behaving in the expected way; (c) interview schedules to determine parent and community opinion about the need for a change or the impact of a change; (d) data from standardized tests to determine how well students have learned over a given period of time in a given subject(s) area(s).

2. *Did your internship projects meet the specific needs of all the individuals who participated?* Where Question 1 focuses on the project goals and objectives of your internship, this question focuses on the needs of individual participants. You must remember that the data you need to answer this question most often must be collected at the time individuals are receiving service. You cannot wait until the end of your internship to survey individuals you might have served at the beginning of your internship.

How well do you believe individual participants' needs were met by your efforts throughout your internship?

_____

_____

_____

_____

_____

3. *Did your internship help to bring about meaningful organizational change in the school building?* Many times internship projects are designed to facilitate the development and implementation of a new program either for the delivery of instructional services to student or to help in the management of the organization. Did your internship facilitate such conditions at the building level?

_____

_____

_____

_____

_____

One important way to determine the answer to this question is to investigate whether or not your internship projects had an impact on the building mission statement. You also might want to ask staff and administration if their individual missions and/or visions regarding schooling and learning were affected by your work.

4. *Did your internship help to bring about meaningful organizational change in the school district?* There are times when an internship project(s) is piloted at a building site with the intention that if it works, the district will adopt it at other building sites. For example, a new discipline approach such as peer mediation might be experimented with at an intern's building site (with the intern leading the pilot effort). If the peer mediation process proves to be successful, it is migrated to other buildings. Thus a pilot project could have an impact on the organizational change of the entire school district.

To what extent do you believe your internship had an impact on the school district?

_____

_____

_____

_____

_____

_____

To examine the answer to this question on a broader base, you might want to review the district's mission statement. Perhaps the board of education presents an annual goals report to the community. You might look at such a document to see if any of your successful projects related to a desired change.

5. *Did your internship provide project participants an opportunity to have input into the overall assessment of the experience?* Did you give staff members, parents, students (where applicable), and community members an appropriate opportunity to let you know how they think your internship affected the district, building, and/or instructional programs? It is important that you get this type of feedback from those who participated in your work but who did not have an official say in the final assessment of your effort. After all, these are the individuals who will be directly affected by your internship. How have you provided for such feedback?

_____

_____

_____

_____

_____

_____

_____

There are many areas that can be assessed in an internship. We have suggested some of the major areas, above. Here are a few more that you might consider, based on the design of your individual program.

- Efforts to bring members of different groups together to work on achieving similar goals and objectives
- Strategies used to engage members from different factions (parents, senior citizens, local government) in project work and support
- Different types of planning strategies
- Innovative strategies for delivering services and products
- Different ways to handle local issues that might be barriers to change

Assessing and Evaluating the Effectiveness of the Intern

Self-Assessment and Self-Evaluation. Ultimately, your field and university mentors will evaluate your success as an administrative intern. However, there are ways for you to continually assess your progress. This will help you make any appropriate midcourse corrections that might afford you a greater amount of success. There are two specific ways that we would recommend: (a) assessing your progress against a list of leadership skills and competencies, and (b) assessing your leadership attitude and behavior as described in your interactive-reflective journal.

Assessing Your Progress Against a List of Leadership Skills and Competencies. During the planning stages of your internship, you should identify those specific leadership skills that you intend to extend and enhance. This should be done on a project-by-project basis. For example, if you are going to develop a better communication device to inform parents about what is taking place in the school building, you will want to identify specific leadership skills and competencies that will be challenged by such a project. Thus, during the course of implementing the project you will be able to monitor your progress in mastering these skills.

We cite a number of different leadership skills and competencies below. At the beginning of your internship, circle "I" for those skills and competencies that you *intend* to enhance and extend throughout your experience. At the end of your internship experience, circle "M" for those skills and competencies that you believe you *mastered*. For each skill and competency that you successfully master, state the reasons why you believe you did so.

Leadership Skills

1. Identify, reflect upon, and articulate ethical beliefs and values   I   M

     Why do you believe you have mastered this skill?

_____

_____

_____

2. Apply various leadership theories appropriately   I   M

     Why do you believe you have mastered this skill?

_____

_____

_____

3. Articulate personal vision in a school mission statement   I   M

     Why do you believe you have mastered this skill?

_____

_____

_____

4. Apply human relations skills when interacting with others   I   M

     Why do you believe you have mastered this skill?

_____

_____

_____

5. Analyze and solve problems using decision-making techniques   I   M

     Why do you believe you have mastered this skill?

_____

_____

_____

6. Develop leadership in others   I   M

Why do you believe you have mastered this skill?

_____

_____

_____

7. Initiate and manage change as a leader   I   M

Why do you believe you have mastered this skill?

_____

_____

_____

8. Initiate and manage change as a member of a leadership team   I   M

Why do you believe you have mastered this skill?

_____

_____

_____

Communication Skills

1. Motivate staff to support the school's mission   I   M

Why do you believe you have mastered this skill?

_____

_____

_____

2. Motivate parents to support the school's mission   I   M

Why do you believe you have mastered this skill?

_____

_____

_____

3. Motivate students to support the school's mission   I   M

Why do you believe you have mastered this skill?

_____

_____

_____

4. Produce clear, articulate written communications   I M

    Why do you believe you have mastered this skill?

_____

_____

5. Analyze the impact of your nonverbal communication   I M

    Why do you believe you have mastered this skill?

_____

_____

6. Listen actively and respond appropriately to others   I M

    Why do you believe you have mastered this skill?

_____

_____

7. Use effective public relations strategies   I M

    Why do you believe you have mastered this skill?

_____

_____

Group Process Skills

1. Facilitate shared decision making   I M

    Why do you believe you have mastered this skill?

_____

_____

2. Enhance staff self-esteem through group activities   I M

    Why do you believe you have mastered this skill?

_____

_____

3. Use conflict resolution techniques   I M

   Why do you believe you have mastered this skill?

_____

_____

_____

4. Plan and conduct effective meetings   I M

   Why do you believe you have mastered this skill?

_____

_____

_____

Curriculum Skills

1. Apply principles of effective curriculum development   I M

   Why do you believe you have mastered this skill?

_____

_____

_____

2. Reinforce the teaching of skills in the school curriculum   I M

   Why do you believe you have mastered this skill?

_____

_____

_____

3. Involve appropriate staff in curriculum development activities   I M

   Why do you believe you have mastered this skill?

_____

_____

_____

4. Promote the teaching of a nondiscriminatory curriculum   I M

   Why do you believe you have mastered this skill?

_____

_____

_____

5. Facilitate the acquisition of curriculum materials and resources   I   M

    Why do you believe you have mastered this skill?

_____

_____

_____

6. Incorporate state mandates in school curriculum   I   M

    Why do you believe you have mastered this skill?

_____

_____

_____

Instructional Skills

1. Recognize, encourage, and monitor effective teaching skills   I   M

    Why do you believe you have mastered this skill?

_____

_____

_____

2. Apply principles of teaching and learning in decision making   I   M

    Why do you believe you have mastered this skill?

_____

_____

_____

3. Use principles of child growth and development   I   M

    Why do you believe you have mastered this skill?

_____

_____

_____

Performance Skills

1. Apply management behaviors that enhance school performance   I M
   Why do you believe you have mastered this skill?

   _____

   _____

   _____

2. Facilitate professional development programs   I M
   Why do you believe you have mastered this skill?

   _____

   _____

   _____

3. Create professional development opportunities for staff   I M
   Why do you believe you have mastered this skill?

   _____

   _____

   _____

4. Identify support services to enhance student performance   I M
   Why do you believe you have mastered this skill?

   _____

   _____

   _____

5. Identify support services to enhance teacher performance   I M
   Why do you believe you have mastered this skill?

   _____

   _____

   _____

6. Create a school climate that enhances school performance   I M
   Why do you believe you have mastered this skill?

   _____

   _____

   _____

Evaluation Skills

1. Apply effective strategies for assessing school programs   I M

 Why do you believe you have mastered this skill?

_____

_____

_____

2. Involve community in assessing progress toward school goals   I M

 Why do you believe you have mastered this skill?

_____

_____

_____

3. Apply effective strategies for evaluating students   I M

 Why do you believe you have mastered this skill?

_____

_____

_____

4. Use effective techniques to enhance the quality of instruction   I M

 Why do you believe you have mastered this skill?

_____

_____

_____

5. Assist staff in the development of professional improvement plans I M

 Why do you believe you have mastered this skill?

_____

_____

_____

Organizational Management Skills

1. Utilize the practical applications of organizational theory   I M

 Why do you believe you have mastered this skill?

_____

_____

_____

2. Use strategic planning skills in managing change   I M

   Why do you believe you have mastered this skill?

_____

_____

_____

3. Develop procedures that comply with federal and state laws   I M

   Why do you believe you have mastered this skill?

_____

_____

_____

4. Develop procedures that comply with contractual agreements   I M

   Why do you believe you have mastered this skill?

_____

_____

_____

5. Understand recruiting practices that attract qualified personnel   I M

   Why do you believe you have mastered this skill?

_____

_____

_____

6. Utilize current technology to assist building management   I M

   Why do you believe you have mastered this skill?

_____

_____

_____

7. Utilize current technology to assist instructional management   I M

   Why do you believe you have mastered this skill?

_____

_____

_____

8. Apply educational law in school practices   I M

    Why do you believe you have mastered this skill?

_____

_____

_____

9. Understand the procedures for managing the school physical plant I M

    Why do you believe you have mastered this skill?

_____

_____

_____

Fiscal Management Skills

1. Understand effective budget management practices   I M

    Why do you believe you have mastered this skill?

_____

_____

_____

2. Apply basic principles of financial management   I M

Why do you believe you have mastered this skill?

_____

_____

_____

3. Understand the procedures for developing a school budget   I M

Why do you believe you have mastered this skill?

_____

_____

_____

Political Management

1. Analyze and understand how to use a community power structure   I   M

   Why do you believe you have mastered this skill?

   _____

   _____

   _____

2. Act effectively within the politics of school district decision making   I   M

   Why do you believe you have mastered this skill?

   _____

   _____

   _____

3. Understand the relationship between local politics and school issues   I   M

   Why do you believe you have mastered this skill?

   _____

   _____

   _____

4. Understand the relationship between state politics and school issues   I   M

   Why do you believe you have mastered this skill?

   _____

   _____

   _____

5. Understand the relationship between national politics and school issues   I   M

   Why do you believe you have mastered this skill?

   _____

   _____

   _____

There are many more skills that you should seek to extend and enhance during your internship experience. Perhaps there are some that are unique to your particular situation. Take a few moments to think about what they might be and list them below:

Skill definition: _____   I   M

Why do you believe you have mastered this skill?

_____

_____

_____

Skill definition: _____   I   M

Why do you believe you have mastered this skill?

_____

_____

_____

Skill definition: _____   I   M

Why do you believe you have mastered this skill?

_____

_____

_____

Skill definition: _____   I   M

Why do you believe you have mastered this skill?

_____

_____

_____

Skill definition: _____   I   M

Why do you believe you have mastered this skill?

_____

_____

_____

Skill definition: _____   I   M

Why do you believe you have mastered this skill?

_____

_____

_____

Skill definition: _____   I   M

Why do you believe you have mastered this skill?

_____

_____

_____

Assessing Your Leadership Attitude and Behavior as Described in Your In-teractive-Reflective Journal. As previously stated, your interactive-reflective journal is extremely important to your success in the internship. If you routinely, clearly, and articulately describe your true feelings about what is happening, it will provide an excellent record of information.

One of the useful products that can emerge from an interactive-reflective journal is data relating to your leadership attitude and behavior. When you begin your internship you will have very tentative feelings about how to act in your new environment. This is common and quite similar to starting a new job. Your initial journal entries will more than likely address your uneasy feelings.

Can you project what your feelings about leadership might be like on the first day of your internship? How might you describe these feelings in your interactive-reflective journal?

_____

_____

_____

_____

_____

_____

As your internship progresses, you will observe school administrators performing their daily operational tasks. This experience will help you decide how you might approach the same tasks. In some instances, you will agree with what you observe. In other instances, you will disagree with what you observe. As you record your observations in your journal, you will candidly describe your true feelings about how building administrators function in their jobs. You will also indicate how you would approach similar tasks. These writings will help you define the real expectations you hold for yourself as a practicing school administrator.

Can you project what your feelings about leadership might be like on the last day of your internship? How might you describe these feelings in your interactive-reflective journal?

_____

_____

_____

_____

_____

_____

As you proceed through your internship period, your interactive-reflective journal should reflect how you are developing into the effective school administrator that you would like to become. If these are the types of comments you are making, a periodic review of your interactive-reflective journal will help you make a self-assessment of your progress. You may want to discuss these reflections with your field mentor, university mentor, and/or your peers who are engaged in their own internships. Their feedback could create a combination of data to provide you with excellent ideas for adjusting your leadership attitudes and behaviors.

University and Field Mentor Evaluations of the Intern

An important part of your mentors' roles in your internship is to provide you with continuous feedback about the progress of your leadership performance. This is accomplished in two ways: (a) on-site observations when you are engaged in a responsible leadership task and (b) written reports of their perceptions of your work.

On-Site Observations of Your Performance. You should seek continuous feedback from your mentors regarding your actual performance. Some of the richest information you can receive is one-on-one mentor feedback immediately after you have performed at your internship site. These observations can be, for example, of your leading a committee meeting, communicating with parents, or giving a report to the board of education.

When your field mentor observes you, it is important that he or she record such information as: (a) whether your procedures were correct for the particular situation, (b) how you might have been more effective, (c) whether you achieved the mission of your task, and (d) whether your performance was culturally acceptable to the organization. Your field mentor should be able to comment on each of these items from a site-specific, practical point of view. You can then use this feedback with some immediacy to modify your behavior and enhance your performance.

When your university mentor observes you, it is important that he or she record such information as: (a) whether you were cognizant of translating theory into practice when you were performing, (b) whether you proceeded within your internship planning proposal, (c) whether there were alternative strategies or procedures that you could have used to enhance your success, and (d) whether you achieved the mission of your task. Your university mentor should be able to provide you with critical insights into these important performance areas.

Written Evaluations of Your Performance. It is extremely important that your development as an effective school administrator be documented from time to time. In many internship programs, written evaluations are used as summative statements, that is, at the very end of the experience. However, we suggest that you receive at least two written evaluations from your field mentor during the course of your internship experience. One of these written evaluations should be conducted at the halfway point of your experience. The other should be at the end of it. In this way you will have documented evidence of your progress, as well as a written guide that you can return to as you move toward the end of your internship. At the end of your experience you will be able to do a comparative analysis of both evaluations.

There are many types of written evaluation forms that could be used to monitor your progress during your internship period. We suggest that the instrument that is used carefully parallels the skills program you committed to when you started your internship. The items in the instrument in Figure 9.1 are offered as illustrations of the skills that should be assessed in writing. They correspond to the standards adopted by the National Association of Secondary School Principals (as mentioned in Chapter 5). These standards are correlated to generic skills that should be included in any internship encounter. They are also part of the evaluation instrument used by the Department of Educational Leadership at Rowan University in Glassboro, New Jersey.

In addition to the skill areas in Figure 9.1, there are other areas that mentors can comment on:

(text continues on page 156)

Figure 9.1. Evaluation Items for a School Administrative Internship

---

PROBLEM ANALYSIS:

Ability to seek out relevant data and analyze complex information to determine the important elements of a problem situation; searching for information with a purpose.

/_____ /_____

| High | High Average | Average | Low Average | Low | Not Observed |

Comment: _____

_____

_____

JUDGMENT:

Ability to reach logical conclusions and make high-quality decisions based on available information; skills in identifying educational needs and setting priorities; ability to evaluate critically written communications.

/_____ /_____

| High | High Average | Average | Low Average | Low | Not Observed |

Comment: _____

_____

_____

ORGANIZATIONAL ABILITY:

Ability to plan, schedule, and control the work of others; skill in using resources in an optimal fashion; ability to deal with a volume of paperwork and heavy demands on one's time.

/_____ /_____

| High | High Average | Average | Low Average | Low | Not Observed |

Comment: _____

_____

_____

(continued)

Figure 9.1. Continued

DECISIVENESS:

Ability to recognize when a decision is required (disregarding the quality of the decision) and to act quickly.

/_____ /_____

| High | High Average | Average | Low Average | Low | Not Observed |

Comment: _____

_____

_____

LEADERSHIP:

Ability to get others involved in solving problems; ability to recognize when a group requires direction; ability to interact with a group effectively and to guide them to the accomplishment of a task.

/_____ /_____

| High | High Average | Average | Low Average | Low | Not Observed |

Comment: _____

_____

_____

SENSITIVITY:

Ability to perceive the needs, concerns, and personal problems of others; skill in resolving conflicts; tact in dealing with persons from different backgrounds; ability to deal effectively with people concerning emotional issues; knowing what information to communicate and to whom.

/_____ /_____

| High | High Average | Average | Low Average | Low | Not Observed |

Comment: _____

_____

_____

Figure 9.1. Continued

STRESS TOLERANCE:

Ability to perform under pressure and during opposition; ability to think on one's feet.

/_____ /_____

High		High	Low		Not
High	Average	Average	Average	Low	Observed

Comment: _____

_____

_____

ORAL COMMUNICATION:

Ability to make a clear oral presentation of facts or ideas.

/_____ /_____

High		High	Low		Not
High	Average	Average	Average	Low	Observed

Comment: _____

_____

_____

WRITTEN COMMUNICATION:

Ability to express ideas clearly in writing, and to write appropriately for different audiences (students, teachers, parents).

/_____ /_____

High		High	Low		Not
High	Average	Average	Average	Low	Observed

Comment: _____

_____

_____

(continued)

Figure 9.1. Continued

RANGE OF INTEREST:

Competence to discuss a variety of subjects (educational, political, current events issues); desire to participate actively in events.

/_____ /_____

| | High | | Low | | Not |
| High | Average | Average | Average | Low | Observed |

Comment: _____

_____

_____

PERSONAL MOTIVATION:

Evidences need to achieve in all activities attempted; evidence that work is important to personal satisfaction; ability to be self-policing.

/_____ /_____

| | High | | Low | | Not |
| High | Average | Average | Average | Low | Observed |

Comment: _____

_____

_____

EDUCATIONAL VALUES:

Possession of a well-reasoned educational philosophy; receptiveness to new ideas and change.

/_____ /_____

| | High | | Low | | Not |
| High | Average | Average | Average | Low | Observed |

Comment: _____

_____

_____

Figure 9.1. Continued

ABILITY TO DEMONSTRATE VISION:

/_____ /_____

Always   Usually   Sometimes   Never   Not
Demonstrated   Demonstrated   Demonstrated   Demonstrated   Observed

ABILITY TO THINK AND ACT CREATIVELY AND INNOVATIVELY:

/_____ /_____

Always   Usually   Sometimes   Never   Not
Demonstrated   Demonstrated   Demonstrated   Demonstrated   Observed

ABILITY TO MOTIVATE AND INSPIRE OTHERS:

/_____ /_____

Always   Usually   Sometimes   Never   Not
Demonstrated   Demonstrated   Demonstrated   Demonstrated   Observed

ABILITY TO LISTEN AND EVIDENCE SENSITIVITY TO OTHERS'
NEEDS AND CONCERNS:

/_____ /_____

Always   Usually   Sometimes   Never   Not
Demonstrated   Demonstrated   Demonstrated   Demonstrated   Observed

ABILITY TO INITIATE AND BE ASSERTIVE:

/_____ /_____

Always   Usually   Sometimes   Never   Not
Demonstrated   Demonstrated   Demonstrated   Demonstrated   Observed

ABILITY TO BE A DECISIVE RISK TAKER AND PROBLEM SOLVER:

/_____ /_____

Always   Usually   Sometimes   Never   Not
Demonstrated   Demonstrated   Demonstrated   Demonstrated   Observed

(continued)

Figure 9.1. Continued

ABILITY TO PLAN:

/_____ /_____

Always	Usually	Sometimes	Never	Not
Demonstrated	Demonstrated	Demonstrated	Demonstrated	Observed

ABILITY TO ORGANIZE:

/_____ /_____

Always	Usually	Sometimes	Never	Not
Demonstrated	Demonstrated	Demonstrated	Demonstrated	Observed

ABILITY TO DELEGATE:

/_____ /_____

Always	Usually	Sometimes	Never	Not
Demonstrated	Demonstrated	Demonstrated	Demonstrated	Observed

ABILITY TO COORDINATE:

/_____ /_____

Always	Usually	Sometimes	Never	Not
Demonstrated	Demonstrated	Demonstrated	Demonstrated	Observed

ABILITY TO ALLOCATE RESOURCES:

/_____ /_____

Always	Usually	Sometimes	Never	Not
Demonstrated	Demonstrated	Demonstrated	Demonstrated	Observed

- Curriculum and evaluation
- Instruction and supervision
- Student services
- Student personnel management
- Community relations
- Student relations
- Facility management

- School finance
- School law
- Technical knowledge/skills
- Technology
- Business management

Summary

In this chapter, we have alluded to various evaluation processes that can be used to assess interns' progress during their internship period. It is important to remember that while your mentors are your official evaluators, you are also responsible for conducting self-evaluations of your progress. It is also important to remember that evaluation instruments should parallel the skills in your initial program design. Evaluation and assessment are important necessities for informing you about your progress toward becoming an effective school administrator.

CHAPTER **10**

After the Internship

What's Next?

From the Field 10.1

Bridget Spencer had had a great time for the past 8 years as a classroom teacher. She loved working with her primary grade students in her school on the west side of a medium-sized midwestern city. But ever since she began her career, she had wanted to follow in her father's footsteps and become an elementary school principal. As a result, she spent a lot of time and effort during the past 4 years enrolling as a part-time student in the masters' degree program in educational administration at Carson Tech University where she earned not only a graduate degree, but most important, her state principal's certificate. Within a few months of completing that goal, she was overjoyed to get a call from a neighboring school district where she had applied for several administrative openings. They were inviting her to become the assistant principal at Benton Hills Elementary School, a small grade K through 4 building in a poor section of the community. It was not going to be a glamorous job, but it was going to be her first step toward the principalship at some point in the future.

As she began to prepare herself for the new job, she could not help but begin to reflect on the preparation program that she had gone through at Carson Tech. She really enjoyed the supervision course, and she also had learned quite a bit in the law course and the required course in human relations. She did not have many kind words to say about the finance or personnel courses, but she "survived" both and moved on to the one thing that she really felt gave her some insights and confidence in being a principal some day. That experience was the internship. At first, she thought it was a huge pain in the neck; she had to teach her full load of classes every day, then spend any free time and planning periods she had working with Erin Montoya, her principal and field mentor for the internship. She also had to spend time every 2 weeks in seminars with the other Carson interns that term. It took a lot of time, but she really felt that the experience out in the field had given

158

her some important insights that she now took with her to her new job. Although she grew up in a principal's household, she felt that the time as an intern had been a learning experience that now made her ready to walk into her new school with confidence.

We hope that everyone who goes through the internship at a university can share the same feelings that Bridget Spencer does in the scenario above. We hope that finishing the internship does not signal the end of something that you endured for the sake of getting a piece of paper from the state department of education. We hope that you are now beginning to feel as if you can really make a difference in the lives of teachers, parents, and, most of all, students because you believe in yourself as a school leader.

Throughout this book, we have described many different ways in which an experience often required for administrator certification may be made into an exciting and effective way to learn about becoming an educational leader. We have suggested some steps that might be followed in planning the administrative internship, and some responsibilities that might be assigned to the university supervisor, administrator field mentor, and of course, the intern. We also noted some of the competency frameworks that might be followed by interns, and also strategies that can be used in evaluating and assessing the learning that takes place during the internship. Throughout the book a consistent assumption has been that the internship is a valuable experience for assisting an aspiring school administrator to learn the requisite skills and practices needed to succeed as a beginning assistant principal or principal. However, we also note that the internship should serve as a foundation for people to move beyond the initial stages of their new careers and become educational leaders.

In this last chapter, our goal is to consider the critical question that really is much more important than how to get through a single learning experience such as the internship. Let us assume that you complete the internship successfully, that you qualify for and obtain an administrative certificate or license in your state, and that you find a job as an administrator. The question we now raise is what you will do for an encore once you get that first position as an assistant principal or principal? What can you bring from the internship experience as a way to help you throughout your future career as an educational leader?

Lessons Learned

As noted throughout the earlier chapters of this book, there are many important benefits to be derived from participation in a well-designed administra-

tive internship. Some of the most powerful features may be the following issues, which we believe can be helpful to you well after you have stepped into
an administrative career in the future.

- The practical experiences of the internship cause interns to become
  more reflective concerning their duties as leaders. Often, effectiveness
  in practice means that persons learn from past behaviors, not simply
  that they always knows the right answers going into situations.

- The internship creates a mind-set that administrators will be more
  successful if they learn to rely on others to address complex issues. No
  one can learn everything necessary to be an effective leader on their
  own; it is a team effort, and that same mind-set will improve practice
  in schools long after interns assume full-time administrative positions.

- In an effective internship, there are always more opportunities for
  questions; answers come slowly. That is the same as it is in the real
  world of administrative practice.

- Internships create a mind-set of continuous learning. The same attitude is critical for effective administrative performance in schools.

- When interns have successful experiences by learning from field mentors, they are more likely to retain that value throughout their professional lives once they become principals or assistant principals.

- Successful internships mean that the quality of life in a school im-
  proves because there is energy present in someone who wants to learn
  about effective practice. Interns who become practicing administrators may keep that sense of vitality going throughout a career.

- Those who have successful learning experiences as interns appreciate
  the complexity of leadership in education because they are able to
  interact with a wide variety of critical performers in schools. The same
  ability will be critical throughout the career of effective educational
  leaders.

- Interns must be learners. Effective principals must always cling to the
  notion that they are effective because they are the "Number One
  Learner" in the school if teachers are to continue learning, and students will learn if teachers continually model the behavior of effective
  learners as well.

Summary

At first view, the internship is a simple way to acquire information. Someone
once said, "All you do in the internship is go out and hang around a principal

for a few weeks, pick up a few tricks now and then, and log in your hours to get the certificate." But as we have shown throughout this book, learning in the field is a much more complex activity than that description. It requires hard work on the part of many people, from the university faculty member who supervises the program, to practicing administrators out in the field who serve as mentors, to the interns themselves. One thing we often forget about the administrative internship is that it is the one part of a preservice program that is dedicated to perhaps the most critical issue associated with learning a new career. It is not a time to learn about administration. It is the one time when a person is able to devote full-time effort to learning how to be an administrator. If that lesson is learned through the kinds of activities and practice we have shared here, it is much more likely that you can learn an even more important lesson. Being an administrator is the easy part; being an effective educational leader is the real goal.

Good luck and have a great future as well as a spectacular present!

Suggested Reading

The primary purpose of this book is to provide users with strategies to ensure that a field-based learning experience can be as effective as possible. As a result, most information presented has concerned the ways in which it is possible to acquire practical skills in the real world of schools, not through theories found in books. However, the ideas in books can also help you prepare to step into the critical world of educational leadership in the near future.

Some books that we recommend reading while you proceed through your internship include the following:

Blase, J., & Blase. J. (1998). *Handbook of instructional leadership: How really good principals promote teaching and learning.* Thousand Oaks, CA: Corwin.

Crow, G. M., & Matthews, J. J. (1997). *Finding one's way: How mentoring can lead to dynamic leadership.* Thousand Oaks, CA: Corwin.

Daresh, J. C., & Playko, M. A. (1997). *The beginning principalship: A practical guide for new school leaders.* Thousand Oaks, CA: Corwin.

Donaldson, G., & Marnik, G. (1995). *As leaders learn: Personal stories of growth in school leadership.* Thousand Oaks, CA: Corwin.

Frase, L., & Streshly, W. (1992). *Avoiding legal hassles: What school administrators really need to know.* Thousand Oaks, CA: Corwin.

Palestini, R. H. (1998). *The ten minute guide to educational leadership.* Lanham, MD: Scarecrow Press.

Pellicer, L. (1998). *Caring enough to lead: Schools and the sacred trust.* Thousand Oaks, CA: Corwin.

Villani, S. (1999). *Are you sure you're the principal? On being an authentic leader.* Thousand Oaks, CA: Corwin.

Wallace, R. C., Jr. (1996). *From vision to practice: The art of educational leadership.* Thousand Oaks, CA: Corwin.

Weller, L. D., & Weller, S. (2000). *Quality human resources leadership.* Lanham, MD: Scarecrow Press.

References

Booth, W. C., Colomb, G. G., & Williams, J. M. (1995). *The craft of research.* Chicago: University of Chicago Press.

Creswell, J. W. (1998). *Qualitative inquiry and research design: Choosing among five traditions.* Thousand Oaks, CA: Sage.

Daresh, John C., & Playko, M. A. (1997). *The beginning principalship: A practical guide for new school leaders.* Thousand Oaks, CA: Corwin.

Hart, A. W. (1990). Effective administration through reflective practice. *Education and Urban Society, 22*(2), 153-167.

Hart, A. W., & Bredeson, P. (1996). *The principalship.* New York: Macmillan.

Hesselbein, F., Goldsmith, M., & Beckhard, R. (Eds.). *The leader of the future.* San Francisco: Jossey-Bass.

Interstate School Leaders Licensure Consortium. (1996). *Standards for school leaders.* Washington, DC: Council of Chief State School Officers.

Kouzes, J. M., & Posner, B. Z. (1995). *The leadership challenge: How to keep getting extraordinary things done in organizations* (chap. 3). San Francisco: Jossey-Bass.

Lortie, D. (1975). *Schoolteacher: A sociological study.* Chicago: University of Chicago Press.

National Association of Elementary School Principals. (1991). *Proficiencies for principals.* Alexandria, VA: Author.

Osterman, K. F., & Kottkamp, R. B. (1993). *Reflective practice for educators: Improving schooling through professional development.* Newbury Park, CA: Corwin.

Rossman, G. B., & Rallis, S. F. (1998). *Learning in the field: An introduction to qualitative research.* Thousand Oaks, CA: Sage.

Turney, C. (1982). *Practicum in teacher education: Research, practice, and supervision.* Sidney: Sidney University Press.

Index

Activity log, 22
Administrative competence, 14-16
Administrative error, 5-6
Administrative internship, 11. *See also*
    Internships
Agreement:
    formal internship, 55
    sample administrative internship, 130
Assessment:
    by field mentor, 111-112, 136-149
    by project participants, 135
    by university supervisor, 136-149
    intern effectiveness, 136-149
    leadership skills and competencies,
        136-148
    self-assessment, 136
    See also Evaluation
Attitudes:
    changing societal, 3
    "I-don't-care," 34

Board of education:
    funding from, 28, 34
    policies, decision making and, 121
    working with, 26-28

Central administration. *See* Districtwide
    administration
Change:
    as administration problem area, 36, 38
    attitude, 3
    meaningful organizational, 134-135
    results of, 4-5
    voluntary, 124
Change agent, 59
Change agent theories, 123

Classroom teacher, focus of, 19
Collaboration:
    with families and community, 78
    with field mentor, 112-113
Collegial learning, internship seminars and,
    92-93
Communication:
    as administration problem area, 36-37
    skills, 85, 138-139
Community, collaborating with, 78-79
Complex problem resolution, 83-85
Confidentiality, 108
Contribution to school, 21
Coordinator, internship. *See* University
    supervisor
Core values, 69-70
Council of Chief State School Officers, 70
Courage, 69
Course titles, 11-12
Craft knowledge, 16
Creswell data collection circle, 49-51
Creswell script, 44
Critical friend, 23
Culture. *See* School culture
Curriculum skills, self-assessment of, 140-141

Data:
    analyzing project, 52-53
    procedures for gathering, 49-51
    recording project, 51
    storing, 51
Data collection:
    Creswell data collection circle, 49-51
    interactive-reflective journal, 127-128
Decision making:
    daily, 84

evaluation item on, 152
reflective practice and, 121
student learning and, 77
Department of Educational Leadership, 150
Development:
  of others, 85
  of self, 86
Developmental pattern:
  skill priorities, 63-65
  task areas, 61-63
Diary:
  of perceptions, 22-23
  See also Journal
Districtwide administration, partnership
    with, 28-29
Diversity, as problem area, 36, 38

Economic system, school administrators
    and, 81
Education, students and, 78-79
Educational administration, master's degree
    programs in, 11
Educational skills, self-assessment of, 143
Educational values, 154
Effective field mentors, 102-105
Effective leadership, 6-7
Effective school administrators, 69
Empirical knowledge, 17
Ethics:
  implications for project, 48
  standard of, 79-80
Evaluation:
  as administration problem area, 36-37
  clause, in internship agreement, 57
  field mentor, 149-156
  formative, 90-91
  items for. *See* Evaluation items
  of instructional programs, 40
  on-site performance, 149-150
  self-, of internship experience, 133-136.
    See also Self-assessment
  university supervisor, 149-156
  written, 150, 156
  See also Assessment
Evaluation items:
  decisiveness, 152
  educational values, 154
  judgment, 151
  leadership, 152
  oral communication, 153
  organizational ability, 151
  personal motivation, 154

problem analysis, 151
range of interest, 153-154
sensitivity, 152
stress tolerance, 153
written communication, 153
Expectations, 120-121
Experiential knowledge, 16

Facility resources, 33
Faculty:
  project co-participants from, 48
  working with school, 31-32
Families, collaborating with, 78
Field mentor:
  as primary supervisor, 56
  building principal as, 30
  characteristics of effective, 102-105
  collaboration and, 112-113
  feedback from, 124, 149-156
  goal and objective setting by, 106
  goals of, 8
  ideal, 104
  performance assessment by, 111-112
  responsibilities of, 105-112
  showcasing intern, 110-111
  teamwork involvement and, 109-110
  weekly meetings with, 107-108
Field-based internship programs, 11-12.
    See also Internships
Field-based learning, as requirement, 15
Financial resources, 33
Fiscal management skills, self-assessment
    of, 145
Formal internship agreement:
  follow-up clause, 57
  intern evaluation clause, 57
  primary supervisor clause, 56
  reports and thesis/dissertation clause, 56
  with school district, 55
Full-time administrative intern, 56

Globalization, 3
Goals:
  formulating organizational, 20
  internship, 7-8, 25-26
  leadership, 67-68
  strategies to achieve, 20-21
  survivorship vs. leadership, 59
  See also Goals and objectives
Goals and objectives:
  internships, 13-24
  reaffirming, 89-90

school year, 20-21
set by field mentor, 106
See also Goals; Objectives
Grade, from university supervisor, 99
Group process skills, self-assessment of,
    139-140

Human resources, 33

Ideal mentor, 104
Insights:
    into professional development, 22-23
    into school, 20-21
Instructional programs:
    data for implementing experimental,
        50-51
    development of, 75-77
    direction of, 82-83
Instructional skills, self-assessment of,
    141-142
Interactive-reflective journal, 127-129
    observations of school administration
        in, 148-149
    self-assessment and, 148-149
Intern:
    as learner, 116-119
    as partner, 119-121
    as reflective practitioner, 121-130
    full-time, 56
    goals of, 7
Internship:
    conditions of, 55-56
    coordination of, 93-97
    current practices, 10-13
    duration of, 13
    expectations and, 120-121
    field-based programs, 11
    follow-up, 57
    goals and objectives, 13-24
    guiding implementation of, 73-74
    in identity crisis, 88
    lessons learned from, 159-160
    projects and activities, 35-38
    timing of, 11
    See also Internship experience
Internship agreement. *See* Formal internship
    agreement
Internship coordinator. *See* University
    supervisor
Internship experience:
    as transitional, 18-19

final outcome of, 69-72. *See also*
    Outcome
goals of, 7-8. *See also* Goals
ingredients of successful, 123
preparedness for, 115
relationships for meaningful, 26-34.
    See also Partnerships
self-evaluation of, 133-136
skill development through, 82
student's assessment of, 12
See also Internship
Internship practice standards, 70-71, 74-82
Internship project proposal:
    design of. *See* Project proposal design
    development questions, 39, 42
    identifying projects and activities, 35-38
    problem areas and, 36
Internship seminars:
    collegial learning and, 92-93
    formative evaluation and, 90-91
    goals of, 88-93
    network building and, 91-92
    reaffirming internship and, 89-90
Interstate School Leaders Licensure
    Consortium (ISLLC), 70-71, 94

Journal, interactive-reflective, 127-129,
    148-149
Judgment skills:
    as evaluation item, 151
    for complex problems, 83

Knowledge:
    developing practical, 72
    forms of, 16-17

Laws, decision making and, 121
Leader, daily routine of, 84
Leadership:
    as evaluation item, 152
    developmental pattern for, 60-65.
        See also Developmental pattern
    effective, 6-7
    goals, 67-68
    influential theories, 123
    moving into, 65-67
Leadership skills:
    assessing competencies and, 136-148
    educational, 82-83
    for 21st century, 70-72
    self-assessment of, 137-138

Learner:
    intern as, 116-119
    willing, 116, 118
Learning by doing, 1, 7, 15, 102, 118-119
Library research, 54
Licensing standards, 70-71
Lifelong learning, 35, 70, 83
Literature review, 54
Log of activities, 22

Management decisions:
    student learning and, 77
    See also Decision making
Material resources, 33
Mentor. *See* Field mentor
Methodology for project implementa-
    tion, 42
Motivation, personal, 154

National Association of Elementary School
    Principals (NAESP), 96
National Association of Secondary School
    Principals (NASSP), 70, 72
    Assessment Center, 96
    standards, 150
National Policy Board for Educational
    Administration, 94
Network building, internship seminar and,
    91-92
Networking relationships, 81

Objectives:
    of internship seminar, 89
    See also Goals and objectives
Observations, on-site, 149-150
Oral communication:
    as evaluation item, 153
    skills, 85
Organizational ability, 84
    as evaluation item, 151
    self-assessment of, 143-145
Outcome:
    final, 69-72
    measuring project's intended, 40
    positive, 14

Partnerships:
    intern in, 119-121
    networks and, 81
    with board of education, 26-28
    with districtwide administration, 28-29
    with school building administration, 29-30

with school faculty, 31-32
    with support staff, 32
Performance skills, self-assessment of, 142
Personal commitment, testing, 18-20, 88
Personal educational platform:
    constructing, 122-125
    defined, 122
    document for, 126
Personal motivation, 154
Planned field experience, 11.
    See also Internship experience;
    Internship
Political implications of project, 48
Political management skills, self-assessment
    of, 146
Political system, school administrators and,
    81
Population, sample, 50
Practicing administrator, 102. *See also* Field
    mentor
Practicum, student teaching, 13-14
Preservice training:
    as requirement, 15
    See also Internship
Principal:
    assigned tasks from, 30
    disciplining adults and, 19
    discussing internship with building, 29-30
    student contact and, 19
Priorities, balancing, 28
Problems:
    analysis of, as evaluation item, 151
    complex, 70
    resolving complex, 83-85
Professional development, insights into,
    22-23
Professional Development Inventory, 96
Proficiencies for Principals (NAESP), 96
Project proposal design, 38-54
    changing during implementation, 54-55
    clarity in, 43
    Creswell script for, 44
    data analysis, 52-53
    data gathering procedures, 49
    development questions, 39, 42
    implementation task list, 53
    literature review in, 54
    project importance, 45-46
    project intent, 43-45
    project limitations, 47
    project problem, 41-43
    project questions, 46-47

project site or population, 48-49
    topic definition, 42-43
Projects, self-evaluation of, 134

Range of interest, 154
Record, activity. *See* Log of activities
Reflective practice, 121-130
    conducting, 126-130
    decision making and, 121
    defined, 122
    interactive-reflective journal and,
        127-128
Reports, responsibility for, 56
Research:
    library, 54
    on theories, 18
Resources:
    acquiring essential, 32-34, 27
    community, 79
    denial of necessary, 39
    facility, 33
    financial, 33
    human, 33
    material, 33
    scarce, 77
Results orientation, 84
Risk management, as problem area, 36-37

Sample population, 50
School, insights into, 20-21
School administrator:
    desire to become, 34-35
    effective, 69
    See also Principal
School building administration, partnerships
    with, 29-30
School culture:
    student learning and, 75-77
    understanding of, 116
School district:
    areas of concern, 35
    formal internship agreement with, 55
    internship site and, 117
    networking with neighboring, 81
School reform, successful, 6
"Selecting and Developing the 21st Century
    Principal," 70, 72
Self-assessment:
    interactive-reflective journal and, 148
    leadership skills and competencies,
        136-146
    skill definition and, 147-148

Sensitivity, 69, 83, 152
Social system, school administrators and, 81
Stakeholder groups:
    partnership with, 26-27
    project support and, 40
    See also Partnerships
Standards, Interstate School Leaders
        Licensure Consortium (ISLLC), 70-71,
        74-82
Strengths and weaknesses, understanding
        your, 86
Stress, tolerance for, 153
Student learning:
    school culture and, 75-77
    vision for, 74-75
Student teaching experience, 13-14
Students, view of intern, 125
Supervisor:
    field mentor as primary, 56. *See also*
        Field mentor
    See also University supervisor
Support staff, working with, 32

Teaching colleagues, view of intern, 125
Teamwork:
    field mentor and, 109-110
    skills, 83
Technology, as problem area, 36, 38
Theoretical knowledge:
    applying, 16-18
    defined, 17
Theories:
    change agent, 123
    practicing espoused, 124
Tradition, 5-6

University educational administration
        programs:
    as recent developments, 15
    multiple audiences for, 11
University faculty supervisor. *See* University
        supervisor
University supervisor:
    feedback from, 124, 149-156
    goals of, 7-8
    grade assignments by, 99
    individual needs and, 96-97
    internship coordination and, 93-97
    involvement of, 12
    positive relationship with, 102
    site visits by, 98

specific duties, 97-99
state requirement knowledge by, 94
university requirements and, 95
Unplanned events, 107

Values:
core, 69-70
educational, 154
nonnegotiable internship, 125
Visibility, increasing, 23

Vision for student learning, 74-75
Visionaries, 70
Voluntary change, 124

Willing learner, 116, 118
Written communication:
as evaluation item
skills, 85
Written evaluations, 150, 156

CORWIN
PRESS

The Corwin Press logo—a raven striding across an open book—represents the happy union of courage and learning. We are a professional-level publisher of books and journals for K–12 educators, and we are committed to creating and providing resources that embody these qualities. Corwin's motto is "Success for All Learners."